"Through two world wars, the cold war, wars of words, wars of nerves, and wars of ideology, President Harry S. Truman kept his crusty sense of humor. Although he offended many with salty language, Truman's plain-speaking style, by today's standards, is a refreshing contrast to the more sophisticated double-talk to which Americans have been accustomed since. He was an uncommonly ordinary and yet extraordinarily uncommon man. What would Harry Truman say if he were here today? Just what he was saying half a century ago . . ."

—Alex Ayres, editor of
The Wit and Wisdom of Harry S. Truman

"You don't get any double-talking from me. I'm either for something or against it, and you know it. You know what I stand for."

"Right has might."

"The greatest orators understood what they wanted to say, said it in short sentences and said it quickly and then got out of there before the people fell asleep."

"I don't believe that because peace is difficult, war is inevitable."

D0802578

ALEX AYRES, a screenwriter and an editor at *Running Times* and the *Harvard Lampoon*, has edited six previous *Wit and Wisdom* titles for Meridian. He lives in Valencia, California.

The Wit and Wisdom

— *Of* —

HARRY S. TRUMAN

EDITED BY
Alex Ayres

A MERIDIAN BOOK

MERIDIAN
Published by the Penguin Group
Penguin Putnam Inc., 375 Hudson Street, New York, New York 10014, U.S.A.
Penguin Books Ltd, 27 Wrights Lane, London W8 5TZ, England
Penguin Books Australia Ltd, Ringwood, Victoria, Australia
Penguin Books Canada Ltd, 10 Alcorn Avenue, Toronto, Ontario, Canada M4V 3B2
Penguin Books (N.Z.) Ltd, 182–190 Wairau Road, Auckland 10, New Zealand

Penguin Books Ltd, Registered Offices:
Harmondsworth, Middlesex, England

First published by Meridian, an imprint of Dutton NAL,
a member of Penguin Putnam Inc.

First Printing, September, 1998
10   9   8   7   6   5   4   3   2   1

Ⓜ REGISTERED TRADEMARK—MARCA REGISTRADA

LIBRARY OF CONGRESS CATALOGING-IN-PUBLICATION DATA:
Truman, Harry S., 1884–1972.
   The wit and wisdom of Harry S. Truman / edited by Alex Ayres.
      p.   cm.
   Includes bibliographical references (p.   ).
   ISBN 0-452-01182-5
   1. Truman, Harry S., 1884–1972—Quotations.   I. Ayres, Alex.
II. Title.
E742.5.T62   1998
973.918—dc21   98-14744
                                                                                      CIP

Printed in the United States of America
Set in Palatino
Designed by Julian Hamer

To the spirit of Independence

THE BUCK STOPS HERE.
   —sign on Harry Truman's
   desk at the White House

Acknowledgments

Thanks to Harry Truman (it goes without saying), to Hugh Rawson (the editor's editor), Arnold Dolin, Tammy Golden, and Janice Braunstein at Penguin Putnam Dutton/Plume; to my literary agent Hy Cohen and my research associate Janine Cooper, and to other unnamed co-conspirators in a vast plot to disseminate more "wit and wisdom" in the world.

ON HARRY TRUMAN

My whole inclination is to predict the election of Thomas E. Dewey by a heavy margin and devote my time and efforts to other things.

—Elmo Roper, prominent pollster, September 9, 1948
(after poll shows Dewey leading Truman 44.2% to 31.4%)

When the death of President Franklin Delano Roosevelt thrust him suddenly into the Presidency in April of 1945 at one of the most critical moments of our history, he met that moment with courage and vision. His farsighted leadership in the postwar era has helped ever since to preserve peace and freedom in the world.

—Richard M. Nixon, thirty-seventh President, 1972

To err is Truman.

—Republican joke circa 1946

Don't shoot our piano player; he's doing the best he can.

—Republican joke circa 1947

What would Truman do if he were alive?

—Republican joke circa 1948

An example of the ability of this society to yield up, from the most unremarkable origins, the most remarkable men.

—Adlai Stevenson III, Democratic presidential candidate (1952, 1956)

The people of the United States love and voted for Harry Truman not because he gave them hell but because he gave them hope.

—Lyndon Johnson, thirty-sixth President, 1965

President Truman is beloved by the American people because of his candor; honesty, frankness, and principle. . . . He represented in the minds of the American citizens the bold principles of the New Deal and the Fair Deal.

—Hubert Humphrey, Vice-President, 1966

Truman presided over the creation of the Western World as it still broadly exists today. The creation of NATO, the Marshall Plan with its emphasis on European unity, the resistance to Soviet expansion, peacefully in Berlin, bloodily in Korea, all had long-lasting consequences. He was a president of great significance.

—Roy Jenkins, *Truman,* 1986

No matter where he was or what he had to do, even in the White House he was never too busy to make a joke.

—Sue Gentry, *Independence Examiner,* 1972

His eye is clear and he is just as solid as a wall. His jaw is square and his stomach is just as flat as an athlete's.

—Gene Tunney, ex–heavyweight boxing champion, after a social call on President Truman, 1945

Harry Truman proves the old adage that any man can become President of the United States.

> —Norman Thomas, Socialist party presidential candidate
> (1928, 1932, 1936, 1940, 1944, 1948)

I have never understood why the press did such an abysmally poor job in writing about the President. . . . I have read over and over again that he was an *ordinary* man. Whatever that means . . . I consider him one of the most extraordinary human beings who ever lived.

> —Dean Acheson, Secretary of State (1949–1953), 1969

He is a malignant, scheming sort of an individual who is dangerous not only to the United Mine Workers, but dangerous to the United States of America.

> John L. Lewis, president, United Mine Workers (1920–1960)

I am ready to hazard an opinion, to which I came, I confess manfully, with dragging feet, that Harry Truman will eventually win a place as President alongside Jefferson and Theodore Roosevelt. . . . He remained more genuinely "home folks" than any other President.

> —Clinton Rossiter, *The American Presidency*, 1956

The memory of him has never been sharper, never brighter than it is now, a time when menacing, shadowy men are everywhere among us.

> —Merle Miller, *Plain Speaking*, 1973

He had had to assume command of the most powerful industrial nation on earth at the very moment when that power, in combination with stunning advances in science and technology, had become an unparalleled force in the world. The responsibilities he bore were like those of no other president before him, and he more than met the test.

> —David McCullough, *Truman*, 1992

The national security state was Truman's true gift to future generations. It helped to stabilize the capitalist, liberal society.

—William Pemberton, *Harry S. Truman:*
Fair Dealer and Cold Warrior, 1989

He can already be called the most underrated President in this country's entire history.

—Alfred Steinberg, *The Man from Missouri*, 1962

The Presidents now considered great were not always so regarded when they took office or even when they left it. Abraham Lincoln was one of them—Harry Truman is now another.

—John Hollister Hedley,
Harry S. Truman: the "Little" Man from Missouri, 1979

And yet where Lincoln saved a nation, Truman saved a world.

—William S. White, *The Responsibles*, 1972

. . . a great, great President. As time goes on the greatness of his personality and his actions will become more apparent to the nation and the world.

—Earl Warren, Chief Justice of the Supreme Court (1953–1969;
Republican vice-presidential candidate, 1948)

Possibly the best President of this century. . . . What the Presidents we remember are remembered for is leadership in time of peril. Washington led us in the peril of birth; Jefferson in the peril of an emerging government . . . Lincoln guided us through . . . desperate times in our history; Teddy did the same; and that brings us to Truman.

—Senator Barry Goldwater
(Republican presidential candidate), 1964

Since Harry Truman left town almost nobody has spoken his mind. Mr. Truman took the tradition of plain speaking back to Missouri with him.

—Mary McGrory, Washington writer

As late as the 1970's, the self-deprecatory "folk humor" of the late Harry S. Truman and Senator Sam Ervin not only amused millions of Americans but also won their hearty praise.

—Walter Blair and Hamlin Hill, *America's Humor,* 1978

Truman was the last authentic American, with all the characteristic faults and virtues of the breed, to occupy the White House, and I doubt very much if there will ever be another.

—Malcolm Muggeridge, British writer–commentator

He was a great man, yes, but he has given us a gift that we do not always get from great men—he gave us the gift of warm, smiling memories.

—Senator Philip Hart

I'm ashamed to admit it now, but we used to call Harry a sissy. He wore glasses and didn't play our games. He carried books, and we'd carry a baseball bat.

—Morton Chiles, childhood neighbor of Harry Truman

They say they knew it all along, his becoming President— but nobody did. Nobody thought that he'd go far at all.

—Miss Zuba Chiles, childhood schoolteacher

The last time you and I sat across the conference table was at Potsdam, Mr. President. I must confess, sir, I held you in very low regard then. I loathed your taking the place of

Franklin Roosevelt. I misjudged you badly. Since that time, you, more than any other man, have saved Western civilization.

—Winston Churchill, in a toast to Harry Truman, 1953

INTRODUCTION

"Who are you voting for?" Harry Truman called out to a man at a train station during his 1948 "whistle-stop" tour.

The man snapped: "I wouldn't vote for you if you were the only one on the ballot!"

Truman turned to one of his aides and said, "Put that man down as doubtful."

A sense of humor is a distinct advantage, if not a survival trait, for a leader in a democratic society.

Harry Truman kept his crusty sense of humor through some of the greatest crises in history—two world wars, the Cold War, the Korean War, wars of words, wars of nerves, and wars of ideology.

During his pivotal presidency, while negotiating some of the greatest turning points in history, Truman enjoyed a regular ritual of choosing an outrageous tie before breakfast to provoke remarks from his wife and daughter ("I usually put on a terrible tie," he explained, "just to get a loud protest from Bess and Margie"). He wore loud shirts, cracked jokes with colleagues, matched wits with reporters, and sprinkled his speech with salty sayings—Trumanisms . . .

- The buck stops here.
- If you can't stand the heat, you better get out of the kitchen.
- I do what I think is right and let them all go to hell.
- Give 'em hell, and if they don't like it, give 'em more hell.
- I never gave them hell, I just tell the truth and they think it's hell.
- You don't get any double-talking from me. I'm either for something or against it, and you know it. You know what I stand for.
- I never sit on a fence. I am either on one side or another.
- Let's not weasel-word it.
- I'm a meat and potatoes man.
- Would you like to meet the Boss?

—introducing his wife Bess

- Would you like to meet the one who bosses the Boss?

—introducing his daughter Margaret

A late bloomer who did not marry until he was thirty-five, Harry Truman did not discover his true vocation in life—politics—until he was nearly forty. He did not run for the Senate until he was fifty. He was sixty-one when he took over the world's most difficult job on April 12, 1945, at the climactic moment of the greatest crisis in recorded human history—World War II. "There have been few men in all history the equal of the man into whose shoes I am stepping," Truman said solemnly on his first day as president. "I pray God I can measure up to the task."

No Vice-President ever had a harder act to follow. When Andrew Johnson succeeded slain Abraham Lincoln in 1865 the Civil War was over: Lee had surrendered to Grant at Appomattox. But when Harry Truman succeeded Franklin Delano Roosevelt in 1945, World War II was not over. The Nazis had not surrendered, nor the Japanese. It was the toughest job in the world, and Truman came into it the worst way—"through the back door," as he would say.

The climactic battles of the Bulge and Iwo Jima, the historic decision to use the atom bomb, the surrender of Germany and Japan, and the U.S. acceptance of the United Nations charter, all these monumental milestones were passed during Harry Truman's first few months on the job as President. The Truman presidency marked the emergence of the United States as a superpower—not only in military terms but in economic terms. (In 1948 the U.S. produced about 41% of the world's goods and services, and accounted for almost half of the world's industrial output.)

It began humbly. Harry Truman did not start out with any obvious advantages in life. Not heir to a prominent name or family fortune, not endowed with dashing good looks, not even possessed of a college degree, he worked his way up slowly from poverty and near-bankruptcy in his twenties and thirties to the Senate in his fifties and the presidency in his sixties. His sense of humor was one of his greatest assets during his long upward journey.

Truman kept his crusty sense of humor through hundreds of press conferences during his seven years and nine months as President. The official transcripts in the *Public Papers of the Presidents of the United States* are speckled with "laughter" notations. Here are a few examples from 1947:

Q. Mr. President, how do you feel about the recent Russian propaganda, like in the newspapers—

THE PRESIDENT. That is just like the propaganda here at home. I am used to it. [*Laughter.*] They got most of their information out of the papers here at home . . .

Q. You said you are for the Missouri Valley Authority Plan?

THE PRESIDENT. I think I said it a dozen times. You want me to put it down in writing and hand it to you? [*Laughter.*]

Q. Mr. President, could we have a clue as to who the four Republicans are you don't like? You are quoted as having said at the last congressional reception that there are only four you don't like.

THE PRESIDENT. Well, I wouldn't like to limit it to four. [*Laughter.*]

Q. Mr. President, have you given any thought to grocery prices?

THE PRESIDENT. I have given it no thought. Only when I go to pay my bill. [*Laughter.*]

Q. Mr. President, are you going to Kentucky about the first of August?

THE PRESIDENT. I don't think so. I have no engagements from now until next Christmas that I know of. [*Laughter.*]

Q. I am curious to know what a high priority at [an] overseas base might be?

THE PRESIDENT: I can't tell you. It's a diplomatic secret, and until we find out ourselves—[*Laughter.*] I will tell you one of these days, but not now.

Q. Mr. President, have you seen any flying saucers?

THE PRESIDENT: Only in the newspapers. [*Laughter.*]

Truman earned a reputation for "plain talking," but Truman did not tell all (no President can tell all). There were omissions, he admitted. "For reasons of national security and out of consideration for some people still alive, I have omitted certain material," he wrote in the preface of his memoirs' second volume, *Years of Trial and Hope* (1956).

"Some of this material cannot be made available for many years, perhaps for many generations."

In the information age there is never a shortage of facts, statements, or opinions, but there is always a shortage of truth. Humor helps break down the barriers to truth. Humor helps restore the rule of common sense.

Harry Truman used humor as a human common denominator for communicating with people. He also used humor as a powerful weapon against the opposition. Truman's clever method of attacking his Republican opponent Thomas Dewey's credibility in the campaign of 1948 was to tell a humorous parable about "Doctor Dewey" (see DOCTOR DEWEY), which proved far more effective than mud-slinging invective.

Harry Truman did not tell all, but after half a century Harry Truman's words still hold truth and humor (or wisdom and wit). Although Truman offended many with his occasional salty language and liberal sprinkling of terms such as "hell," "hooey," "high hats," "stuffed shirts," "s.o.b.," "nincompoop," and "pinhead," sometimes he could not resist using strong language when he felt strongly about something; some of his saltier sayings are among his most passionately heartfelt. Truman's plain-speaking style, by today's standards, is a refreshing contrast to the more sophisticated double-talk and truth-torturing image manipulation to which Americans have since become accustomed. Truman dared to defy the polls and do what he thought was right, even if it was not politically correct or popular.

The quotations in *The Wit and Wisdom of Harry S. Truman* are drawn from public papers, private papers, press conferences, books, letters, notes, memoranda, diary entries, messages to Congress, lectures, memoirs, and speeches. Reference dates after 1972 refer to posthumous publications of Truman materials. None of Truman's words have been altered, but speeches, paragraphs, and sentences have sometimes been abbreviated for quotability; ellipses indicate editing.

The Wit and Wisdom of Harry S. Truman offers an A-to-Z compendium of the best of what Truman had to say on a wide variety of subjects (including the other Presidents); it also includes a brief biography chronicling the highlights of Truman's life. In another way, it can be seen as a character portrait, drawn from his own words, of a twentieth-century narrator of the American odyssey, an uncommonly ordinary and yet extraordinarily uncommon man in whose reflection we see glimpses of our national identity.

What would Harry Truman say if he were here today? Just what he was saying half a century ago is what he is saying to us today.

- Do what you think is right and let them all go to hell.
- I don't care what your politics are, I don't care what you believe politically, and I don't care what your religion is, as long as you live by it and act by it.
- Right Has Might.
- Readers of good books, particularly books of biography and history, are preparing themselves for leadership.
- Not all readers become leaders. But all leaders must be readers.
- Tie on your hat.
- Do your best. History will do the rest.
- There is nothing new in the world except the history you do not know.
- It's what you learn after you know it all that counts.
- Children nowadays have too many gadgets to fool with and not enough chores.
- I've never known hard work to hurt anybody. It's lack of hard work that kills people.
- It's a recession when your neighbor loses his job; it's a depression when you lose your own.

- An economist is a man who wears a Phi Beta Kappa key at one end and no watch at the other.
- Prosperity for us means prosperity for other people.
- You can't make a man good by passing a law that he must be good.
- Women have everything else—why not the presidency?

THE WIT AND WISDOM
OF
HARRY S. TRUMAN

A

ACHESON, DEAN

Secretary of State Dean Acheson offered his resignation to President Truman after the conviction of State Department official Alger Hiss on perjury charges in 1950.

Truman refused to accept the resignation. "In the long run," he told Acheson, "after all the hullaballoo is over, people will remember that you're a man who stuck by his friends, and that's what counts."

Acheson wrote later about that moment:

Then he looked up at me and he said, "Dean, always be shot in front, never behind."

And then he said, "You'd better get back to work. We've got a lot of important work to do."

And, of course, that is what I did, and the matter of my resignation was never mentioned again.

ACORN THINKING

Harry Truman was not an "acorn thinker." He defined this term once in a speech in Missoula, Montana, on May 12, 1950, where he urged the citizens to do something about politicians who specialized in "acorn thinking."

"Some people will take a look at an acorn and all they can see is just an acorn." Others, the President said, "can see into the future. They can see a giant oak tree, with its great limbs spreading upward and outward and coming from that acorn.

"In Washington, there are some men, no matter how hard they try, who can only see little acorns. . . . Even give them a magnifying glass, or even a pair of spyglasses, or even a telescope, they just shake their heads and all they can say is, 'I'm sorry, I can't see anything but an acorn there.' "

ADAMS, JOHN
(U.S. President 1797–1801)

John Adams and Thomas Jefferson both died on the fiftieth anniversary of the Declaration of Independence.

"When Adams died in Quincy, Massachusetts, on July 4, 1826, at about six o'clock in the evening, he was nearly ninety-one, making him the president with the longest life thus far," Truman noted in *Where the Buck Stops*. "His final thoughts were on the United States and on Jefferson; his last words were, 'The country is saved, and Jefferson lives.' But that was also a final irony in the lives of the two men, because Jefferson was already dead. He died five hours before Adams, at twelve-fifty p.m., aged eighty-three."

(see JEFFERSON, THOMAS)

ADAMS, JOHN QUINCY
(U.S. President 1825–1829)

"The single really interesting thing about Adams, I'm afraid," Truman said of the sixth president, "is that he was the only son of a president in our history to become president himself."

ADVANTAGES

"My own sympathy has always been with the little fellow, the man without advantages," Truman wrote in observance of his eightieth birthday, "with no pull at the seat of the mighty."

(see DEMOCRATIC PARTY)

ADVICE

"Always be nice to all the people who can't talk back to you," Truman advised his daughter, Margaret.

Aware that advising one's own children is easy, but getting them to take the advice can be difficult, Truman offered this advice to would-be advice-givers to children:

"I have found the best way to give advice to your children is to find out what they want and then advise them to do it. . . .

"Advice to grandchildren is usually wasted. If the second and third generations *could* profit by the experience of the first generation, we would not be having some of the troubles we have today."

On his eightieth birthday Harry Truman was asked his advice on how to reach four score.

"Pick the right grandparents," he advised reporters, "don't eat or drink too much, be circumspect in all things, and take a two-mile walk every morning before breakfast."

During the campaign of 1964 Truman offered this advice to vice-presidential candidate Hubert Humphrey:

"Carry the battle to them. Don't let them bring it to you. Put them on the defensive. And don't ever apologize for anything."

To young people who aspired to grow up and make history as he had done, Truman offered this simple advice:

"Do your best. History will do the rest."

A good name and good advice is all your dad can give you.
—letter to Margaret Truman, February 6, 1947

Make no little plans. Make the biggest one you can think of, and spend the rest of your life carrying it out.
—found in President's Secretary's files, undated

I don't care what your politics are, I don't care what you believe politically, and I don't care what your religion is, as long as you live by it and act by it.
—*Truman Speaks*, 1960

AFFABILITY

"You must meet contingencies as they arise, and face them squarely," Truman advised Margaret in a letter on her twentieth birthday. "And I'm sure you will. You should have enough of your mother's will power and strength of character and your dad's affability to make out."

AFTERTHOUGHT

I have tried to refrain from hindsight and afterthoughts. Any schoolboy's afterthought is worth more than the forethought of the greatest statesman.
—Preface, *Memoirs*, Vol. 2, 1956

AIM

In short, our fundamental aim was and is to assure the integrity and vitality of the free society we live in, a society that is based upon the dignity and worth of the individual.

—*Memoirs, Vol. 2*, 1956

AMERICA

No nation on this globe should be more internationally minded than America because it was built by all nations.

—remarks, Chicago, March 17, 1945

AMERICAN

There is one thing that Americans value even more than peace. It is freedom. Freedom of worship—freedom of speech—freedom of enterprise. . . . The first two of these freedoms are related to the third. . . . So our devotion to free enterprise has deeper roots than a desire to protect the profits of ownership. It is part and parcel of what we call American.

—speech, March 6, 1947

AMERICAN FAITH

Our American faith—a faith that can be simply stated:

We believe that all men are created equal and that they have the right of equal justice under law.

We believe that all men have the right to freedom of thought and of expression and the right to worship as they please.

We believe that all men are entitled to equal opportunities for jobs, for homes, for good health, and for education.

We believe that all men should have a voice in their Government and that Government should protect, not usurp, the rights of the people.

We shall not, however, finally achieve the ideals for which this Nation was founded so long as any American suffers discrimination as a result of his race, or religion, or color, or the land of origin of his forefathers.

—message to Congress, 1948
(see CIVIL RIGHTS)

AMERICAN REVOLUTION

More than half of the world's population was subject for centuries to foreign domination and economic slavery. The repercussions of the American and French revolutions are just now being felt all around the world.

—Preface, *Memoirs, Vol. 2,* 1956

AMERICANS

Americans are funny birds. They are always sticking their noses into somebody's business which isn't any of theirs. We send missionaries and propagandists to China, Turkey, India, and everywhere to tell those people how to live. Most of 'em know as much or more than we do.

—diary, June 7, 1945

ANCESTORS

I once told [Virginia Senator] Harry Byrd I expected to write a book on the white trash of Virginia and what became of them. I had a man who worked for me on the farm from Grayson County, Virginia, and he said to me one time that he thought there ought to be a lot of good people in Virginia because all the white trash had been emptied into Ohio, Kentucky and Indiana. I told that story to Harry Byrd one time and he didn't think it was funny.

The facts are that the so-called trash are usually the ancestors of our really great men. The ancestor worshipers who stayed in England, France and Spain did not make the Western Hemisphere great. It was the so-called lower classes who wanted to improve their lot who made North & South America and Australia and New Zealand great.

The Lords, Ladies, Counts, Earls and Dukes still have their descendants in the old countries but when something has to be done for their salvation a man "south of the tracks" has to do it, as Pershing and Eisenhower did!

—letter to Columbia Records executive Goddard Lieberson, January 1955 (see DESCENDANTS; EISENHOWER, DWIGHT)

ANNIVERSARY

On their twenty-ninth wedding anniversary, June 28, 1948, Harry Truman wrote his wife:

Dear Bess:

Twenty-nine years! It seems like twenty-nine days.

Detroit, Port Huron, a farm sale, the Blackstone Hotel, a shirt store. County Judge, defeat, Margie, Automobile Club membership drive, Presiding Judge, Senator, V.P., now!

You still are on the pedestal where I placed you that day in Sunday school in 1890. What an old fool I am.

Harry

ANTI-ANYTHING

I don't believe in *anti-anything*. A man has to have a program; you have to be for something, otherwise you will never get anywhere.

—lecture, Columbia University, April 28, 1959

ARMY

"I've always been sorry I did not get a university education in the regular way, but I got it in the Army the hard way," said Truman, who served as a battery captain in World War I, "and it stuck."

(see BIOGRAPHY 1918; COLLEGE)

ART

Truman did not warm up quickly to the art of painter Thomas Hart Benton, although he was a fellow Missourian.

Asked if he would pose for a photograph with the artist, President Truman refused. He wrote to Abraham Bernstein, a representative of Benton's:

"In the first place I know nothing about Art with a capital A, particularly the frustrated brand known as Modern. I don't like Mr. Benton's *Kentuckian* [a painting]. It looks like no resident or emigrant from that great state that I've ever seen.

"Both of my grandfathers were from Kentucky as were both of my grandmothers. . . . They did not look like that long necked monstrosity of Mr. Thomas Hart Benton's. I won't encourage him to do any more horrors like those in Missouri's beautiful capitol."

Truman later changed his mind about the artist, coming to appreciate him more and more. A decade later the ex-president commissioned Thomas Hart Benton to decorate the entrance to the Truman Library in Independence with a large mural, *Independence and the Opening of the West.*

ART GALLERIES

"It is a pleasure to look at perfection," Truman wrote after visiting the Mellon Gallery in Washington, D.C., "and then think of the lazy, nutty moderns. It is like comparing Christ with Lenin."

In 1956 the ex-president played the role of American tourist and gallery-hopper in Europe. On June 21 he wrote in his diary:

Visited the Mauritzhaus, a small art gallery in The Hague. It has some Rembrandts and some of the best Dutch landscape painters. These Dutch painters of portraits and landscapes were artists and geniuses.

They make our modern day daubers and frustrated ham and egg men look just what they are. It is too bad that our age has forgotten those things that make real art appealing— or they are too lazy to take the pains to do real work.

I saw a bronze monstrosity in one of the art galleries and asked the director if it was meant to be a bronze picture of a devil's darning needle, a vicious-looking bug that's scary to look at. The director turned pale and told me it was a modernist conception of love at first sight! Then *I* fainted!

ARTHUR, CHESTER
(U.S. President 1881–1885)

Harry Truman referred to Chester Arthur, twenty-first president of the United States, simply as "the guy with the side whiskers and striped pants."

ASSASSINATION ATTEMPT

There was an assassination attempt on President Truman on the night of November 1, 1950. Two Puerto Rican nationalist gunmen named Torresola and Collazo attacked Blair House in Washington, D.C., while Truman was staying there. Twenty-seven shots were fired by the gunmen before Torresola was shot in the head by Private Leslie Coffelt, a guard who had received two bullet wounds in the chest and stomach from Torresola and died soon afterward. Collazo was shot by the guards in the east booth and captured.

"A President has to expect these things," said Truman philosophically to reporters the next day. The President was asked what he would have done if one of the gunmen had confronted him with weapon in hand.

"Heck," Truman replied, "I would have taken the gun away from him, shoved it up his gullet and pulled the trigger."

(see CAPITAL PUNISHMENT)

ATOM

It will always remain my prayer that the world will come to look upon the atom as a source of useful energy and a source of important healing power, and that there will never again be any need to invoke the terrible destructive powers that lie hidden in the elements.

—*Memoirs, Vol. 2*, 1956

ATOMIC AGE

"Our tribal instinct has not been eliminated by science and invention," Truman wrote in a letter to Dean Acheson on St. Patrick's Day 1954. "We, as individuals, haven't caught up physically or ethically with the atomic age. Will we?"

Now we have the results of two all-out wars covering the whole world to face, and the responsibilities of the Atomic Age to assume. If the world and its people can survive all these outbreaks, not to mention Ghengis Khan and Tamerlane, surely we are now faced with the greatest age in history.

—*The Autobiography of Harry S. Truman*, 1980

ATOMIC BOMB

"It was not an easy decision to make," Truman admitted. "I did not like the weapon. But I had no qualms if in the long run *millions of lives* could be saved. . . .

"General Marshall told me it might cost half a million

American lives to force the enemy's surrender on his home grounds."

In his *Memoirs* Truman assumed full responsibility for the decision.

> The final decision of where and when to use the atomic bomb was up to me. Let there be no mistake about it. I regarded the bomb as a military weapon and never had any doubt that it should be used. The top military advisors to the President recommended its use, and when I talked to Churchill he unhesitatingly told me that he favored the use of the atomic bomb if it might aid to end the war.
>
> In deciding to use this bomb I wanted to make sure that it would be used as a weapon of war in the manner prescribed by the laws of war. That meant that I wanted it dropped on a military target. I had told Stimson [War Secretary] that the bomb should be dropped as nearly as possible upon a war production center of prime military importance.

It is an atomic bomb. It is the harnessing of the basic power of the universe.

> —announcement about atomic bomb, July 28, 1945
> (before Hiroshima bombing)

Almost two months have passed since the atomic bomb was used against Japan. That bomb did not win the war, but it certainly shortened the war. We know that it saved the lives of thousands of American and Allied soldiers. . . .

Never in history has society been confronted with a power so full of potential danger and at the same time so full of promise for the future of man and for the peace of the world.

> —message to Congress, October 3, 1945
> (see BIOGRAPHY 1945)

ATOMIC ENERGY

The discovery of the means of releasing atomic energy began a new era in the history of civilization. . . . It may some day prove to be more revolutionary in the development of human society than the invention of the wheel, the use of metals, or the steam or internal combustion engine. . . . The release of atomic energy constitutes a new force too revolutionary to consider in the framework of old ideas.

—message to Congress, October 3, 1945

I believe that atomic energy should not be used to fatten the profits of big business. I believe that it should be used to benefit all the people.

—remarks, Milwaukee, October 14, 1948

AWAKE

A Doubleday editor visited former President Truman in his hotel room during a New York stay.

Truman, now in his seventies, was sitting beside a table piled with books.

"Do you like to read yourself to sleep at night?" the editor asked.

"No, young man," Truman replied. "I like to read myself *awake*."

AWARD

If somebody throws a brick at me I can catch it and throw it back. But when somebody awards a decoration to me, I am out of words.

—on receiving the Grand Cross of Merit of Austria, May 7, 1964

B

BARKLEY, ALBEN W.

As Truman was departing Union Station on his "whistle-stop" campaign tour in 1948, his running mate, Senator Alben Barkley, offered a few parting words.

"Go out there and mow 'em down!" Barkley bellowed.

Truman waved. "I'll mow 'em down, Alben, and I'll give 'em hell!"

(see HELL)

BARUCH, BERNARD

Bernard Baruch, financier and familiar of FDR, was Truman's choice as American representative on the United Nations Atomic Energy Commission. But Truman grew exasperated with the "arrogant, opinionated" Baruch, saying of him privately: "He wants to run the world, the moon and maybe Jupiter."

BATHTUBS

There's a story around the White House that Mrs. Millard Fillmore brought the first bathtub into the White House. There is also a story in connection with it, that the local medical association in Cincinnati, Ohio, passed a resolution calling Mrs. Fillmore an indecent person because she put a bathtub in the White House. This medical association in Cincinnati said that it was unsanitary, that it was unhealthy, that no person should take all his clothes off at one time. . . . Well, my friends, there has been some progress since that date, and I want to say to you, there are more bathtubs in the White House now than there are in the Benjamin Franklin Hotel.

—speech to American Hospital Association,
Philadelphia, September 16, 1952

BEARD

Every man attempts to grow a beard at least once in his life. Harry Truman tried to grow a beard once but gave it up, he said, because the results were discouragingly asymmetrical. He explained:

"The hair on the right side of my face grew upward and on the left it grew down."

BEING RIGHT

"There are those who suggest that all federal employees must bear the burden of always seeming right in addition to being right," said President Truman, a political leader in a world of appearances where to be or not to be is to seem to be or not to seem to be.

"I go along with this exacting standard," Truman continued. "But I will not allow any man to be punished for not seeming to be right if in fact he is not wrong."

BIG LIE

"If you think somebody is telling a big lie about you," Truman liked to say, "the only way to answer it is with the whole truth."

BILLIONS

A reporter at a press conference, while phrasing a question to the President, made the mistake of saying "millions."

Truman interrupted him. "Three million! You have got to speak in billions when you talk about the budget."

BIPARTISAN

"I don't like bipartisans," Truman confessed. "Whenever a fellow tells me he's bipartisan, I know he's going to vote against me."

BLUNTLY

As you know, I speak plainly sometimes—in fact, I speak *bluntly* sometimes and I am going to speak plainly and bluntly today.

—campaign remarks, Detroit, September 6, 1948

BORED

I can't remember being bored, not once in my whole life. How in the world can you be bored if you have things to think about, which I must say I always have?

—quoted by Merle Miller in *Plain Speaking*, 1973

BOSSES

Harry Truman affectionately called his wife Bess "the Boss" (adding that most married men had bosses at home) and his daughter, Margaret, he introduced as "the one who bosses the Boss" or "the Boss's boss." It was a good-natured Trumanism and the crowds loved it, although his wife and daughter did not.

"We never did get him to stop introducing us this way in spite of numerous demands," wrote Margaret in her biography of her father, *Harry Truman* (1973).

The domestic "bosses" were not to be confused with political "bosses," Truman explained: "When a leader is in the Democratic Party he's a boss, when he's in the Republican party he's nothing but a leader."

BRASS HALO

Ike has a brass halo.

—a campaign speech for Adlai Stevenson, October 1952
(see EISENHOWER, DWIGHT; IKE)

BRITISH

The British were winning the Cold War, observed President Truman:

"Russians distribute lies about us. Our papers lie about and misrepresent the motives of the Russians—and the British outlie and outpropagandize us both."

(see ENGLAND)

BROTHERHOOD

I believe in the brotherhood of man, not merely the brotherhood of white men but the brotherhood of all men before law.

—campaign speech, Sedalia, Missouri, 1940

BUSINESS

While serving as a Jackson County judge, his first elected office, Harry Truman bought new seat covers for his car. The man who sold him the seat covers offered to install them for free if Truman would send him some county work. Truman took out his wallet and said, "I don't do business that way."

BUSINESSMAN

Asked about the political prospects of a prominent businessman, President Truman answered with the voice of experience: "The difficulty with businessmen entering politics, after they have had a successful business career, is that they want to start at the top."

BUSINESSMEN

Businessmen don't elect Presidents, anyway. The common people elect them. I proved that back in 1948.

—remarks, New York City, January 9, 1964

C

CAPITAL PUNISHMENT

Pressed by the press for his views on capital punishment, Truman gave this answer:

"I've never really believed in capital punishment. I commuted the sentence of the fellow who was trying to shoot me to life imprisonment. That's the best example I can give you."

(see ASSASSINATION ATTEMPT)

CARD GAMES

During the vice-presidential campaign, on October 12, 1944, a New Orleans reporter asked Senator Truman about his reputed poker playing.

"Card games?" Truman smiled innocently. "The only game I know anything about is that game—let me see—I don't know what the name is, but you put one card face down on the table and four face up, and you bet."

CASTRO, FIDEL

Well, he'd have thanked me, and we'd have talked awhile, and then as he got up to go, I'd have said to him, "Now, Fidel, I've told you what we'll do for you. There's one thing you can do for me. Would you get a shave and a haircut and take a bath?"

—on how he would have handled Castro
(quoted by Merle Miller in *Plain Speaking*, 1973)

CATS

"You have got yourself into an awful lot of trouble with the cat lovers of America," a reporter told the President at a press conference on February 1, 1947.

"With what?" asked Truman.

"The cat lovers of America . . . I think it was your reference to National Cat Week? You are not against cats?"

The President shook his head. "No. Neutral. I am neutral on cats. Certain sort of cats that I am against, but they have two legs."

CHARACTER ASSASSINS

Truman was infuriated by certain editorial writers in the press whom he called "character assassins."

"Many a great and talented scribbler has sold his soul to these purveyors of 'Character Assassination,'" Truman wrote in a desk note found after his death. "The old Moslem assassins of Mesopotamia have a much better chance of a considered 'judgment' in the end than have these paid mental whores of the controller of our so-called 'free press.' This so-called 'free press' is about as free as Stalin's press. The only difference is that Stalin frankly controlled his, and the publishers and owners of our press are always yapping about the Constitution and suppressing a free press."

(see COLUMNISTS, PRESS)

CHILDREN

"Children nowadays," Harry Truman liked to say, "have too many gadgets to fool with and not enough chores."

Truman felt parents should bear more responsibility for the bad behavior of ill-behaved children and delinquents. "Mama and Papa are more to blame than the kids," Truman said in the Senate, "parents should stay home and raise their children and spend less time in taverns."

CHRISTIANS

I rather think there is an immense shortage of Christian charity among so-called Christians.

—memorandum, 1950

CHRISTMAS

"As you get older, you get tired of doing the same things over and over again, so you think Christmas has changed," Truman wrote in retirement. "It hasn't. It's you who has changed."

CHURCH

"Church was rather dull," President Truman jotted down in his diary on June 1, 1945. "But I had a chance to do some thinking and the time was not wasted. A lot of the world's troubles have been caused by the interpretation of the Gospels and the controversies between sects and creeds. It is all so silly and comes of the prima donna complex again. . . .

"Who is to blame for present conditions but sniveling church members who weep on Sunday, play with whores on Monday, drink on Tuesday, well out to [defraud] the Boss on Wednesday, repent about Friday, and start over on Sunday. . . . I've come to the conclusion myself that church is a very handy place to have a nap in most instances."

(see JESUS, PRAYER, RELIGION)

CHURCHILL, WINSTON

"The greatest public figure of our time," was how Truman described British Prime Minister Winston Churchill, adding: "He was as windy as old Langer [North Dakota Senator William Langer], but he knew his English language and after he'd talked half an hour there'd be at least one gem of a sentence and two thoughts maybe which could have been expressed in four minutes."

Churchill later admitted, during a toast in January 1953, that he was pessimistic when Truman first took over from Roosevelt. "I misjudged you badly," Churchill confessed. "Since that time, you, more than any other man, have saved Western civilization."

Churchill in the end would agree, but he had to make a speech about it first.

—Memoirs, Vol. 1, 1955

CIA

The CIA was set up by me for the sole purpose of getting all the available information to the President. It was not intended to operate as an international agency engaged in strange activities.

—letter to William B. Arthur, managing editor of
Look magazine, June 10, 1964 (see FBI)

CIVIL RIGHTS

President Truman was the first chief executive since Abraham Lincoln to make a major issue of civil rights. In 1946 Truman appointed a commission on the civil rights of African-American citizens, then moved to adopt the commission's recommendations, including reform of the treatment of blacks in the military ("and I expect to put the whole program over before I leave this office because it is right," he said). His Executive Order 8802 abolished segregation in the armed forces.

Many Democrats, including Truman's own mother, warned him it might cost him the 1948 election. In his memoirs he recalled:

> A good many people advised me not to raise this whole question of civil rights. They said it would only make things worse. But you can't cure a moral problem or a social problem by ignoring it.
>
> It is no service to the country to turn away from the hard problems—to ignore injustices and human suffering. It is simply not the American way of doing things. Of course, there are always a lot of people whose motto is "Don't rock the boat." They are so afraid of rocking the boat that they stop rowing. We can never get ahead that way.
>
> If something is wrong, the thing to do is to dig it out, find out why it is wrong, and take sensible steps to put it right. We are all Americans together, and we can solve our hard problems together, including the problem of race relations.

(see AMERICAN FAITH)

CLEVELAND, GROVER
(U.S. President 1885–1889, 1893–1897)

Cleveland was a good president because he was familiar with the powers of an executive, and unlike some of his predecessors, he wasn't afraid to use them.

—Where the Buck Stops (Margaret Truman, ed.), 1989

CLOTHES

There has been a lot written about my clothes. Since I was twenty, I have worn suits made for me by my tailor! When I was in the Senate I was picked as one of the ten best dressed Senators. That was so after I became President. But—the dirty press . . . decided that they couldn't hurt the President by dressing him as he should be, so this character assassination gang started to undress me! They went to the opposite extreme and said I was the worst dressed man in the United States! They lied one time or the other. (They lied both times—I'm neither the best nor the worst dressed man.)

—diary, January 3, 1952
(see PRESS, UNCLOTHED)

COLD

"You sound like you have a cold!" a woman called to Truman as he was speaking from the back platform of a train in Barstow, California, during the "whistle-stop" campaign of 1948.

Truman answered her: "That's because I ride around in the wind with my mouth open."

Soon a sore throat developed and a doctor was summoned. Truman wrote his sister Mary of the cold treatment he received:

"Dr. Graham has just sprayed, mopped and caused me to gargle bad tasting liquids until the throat gave up and got well."

COLLEGE

Although he was denied a college education, Harry Truman made certain his daughter got one. Margaret Truman graduated from George Washington University in May

1946. Her father delivered the commencement address and was awarded an honorary LL.D. degree.

"It took Margaret four years," declared the proud father, "but it only took me four minutes."

COLLEGE KIDS

"You can still do something with high school youths, but the college kids are different," remarked President Truman. "They think they know everything."

COLOR LINE

We can't be leaders of the free world and draw a color line on opportunity.

—interview with Edward R. Murrow, February 2, 1958

COLUMBUS, CHRISTOPHER

"If these Republican orators had been living in Columbus' time, I'm sure they would have been among those who believed the world was flat," President Truman addressed a Columbus Day crowd at New York's Waldorf Astoria in 1952. "In fact, I'm not altogether certain what their views may be on that subject now."

COLUMNISTS

These men who write columns for the classified press sell their writing ability just as the light-(lite?)-of-love ladies sell their bodies to the madam of a bawdy house. They write columns on policy in domestic affairs and on foreign affairs from the rumor source, and as long as the "madam"—the publisher—will pay them for this sort of thing.

—from a note found in Truman's desk after his death
(see PUBLISHERS)

COMMUNICATION

The simplest words make for the best communication.

—Truman, *Mr. Citizen*, 1960

COMMUNISM

"You can't shoot ideas with a gun," said President Truman, expressing his opposition to proposed laws against Communism in the United States. "We will not jail anybody for what he thinks or believes."

You cannot stop the spread of an idea by passing a law against it. You cannot stamp out communism by driving it underground. You can prevent communism by more and better democracy.

—public papers, 1948

You know there was but one idealistic example of Communism. That is described in the Acts of the Apostles.

—letter to Margaret Truman, March 13, 1947
(see DEMOCRACY)

COMMUNIST DICTATORSHIP

Some of our young people and intellectuals seemed attracted to the Russian experiment of setting up a new economy based on Communism. Most of these young people and intellectuals would soon learn that they had been duped into believing that Russia was really trying to create a new kind of social and economic order that would abolish depressions, unemployment, hunger, and war. They soon realized that a colossal hoax was being perpetrated by a group of cruel but skillful fanatics who set up a dictatorship with all the trappings of a state religion.

—*Memoirs, Vol. 2*, 1956

CONGRESS

A President has to decide what to tell Congress—and how much.

"If you tell Congress everything about the world situation, they get hysterical," observed President Truman. "If you tell them nothing, they go fishing."

CONSULTANT

President Truman received more advice from consultants than he could take. "A consultant," he said, "is an ordinary citizen away from home."

COOLIDGE, CALVIN
(U.S. President 1923–1929)

"The man who got more rest than any previous president," was how Truman described Calvin Coolidge. " 'Business as usual' was his motto, although Will Rodgers put it another way: 'Keep Cool with Coolidge and Do Nothing.' "

Truman liked to tell the story of the young lady who sat by President Coolidge at dinner. "She tried all evening to get him into a conversation and all she could get was—yes or no or a grunt. She finally told him that she had made a bet that she could get him to say more than three words during the dinner. He merely said to her—'You lose.' "

COURAGE

The virtue I call courage is not in always facing the foe but in taking care of those at home. . . . A true heart, a strong mind and a great deal of courage and I think a man will get through the world.

—essay in high school composition book, age 16

28

COW PALACE

"Don't worry," said Truman on learning that the Republicans might hold their 1956 convention in San Francisco's Cow Palace. "They'll soon convert the Cow Palace into a hog run."

CRACKPOTS

Crackpots have a right to their opinions, Truman wrote in his *Memoirs*. "Everyone has the right to express what he thinks. That, of course, lets the crackpots in. But if you cannot tell a crackpot when you see one, you ought to be taken in."

L.A. is No. 1 and New York City is No. 2 in the crackpot line in the U.S.A. The reason is that retired farmers from the Appalachians to the Rockies, government clerks on retired pay, busted little business men and other members of a class "who have nothing else to do" gravitate to N.Y. and L.A.

> —diary, 5:00 A.M. Fairmont Hotel, San Francisco, September 12, 1962

CRAPS

Presiding Judge Truman, during his days as a local politician in Jackson County, Missouri, discovered he could pass legislation while his legal colleagues played craps:

"I'd let them start a crap game and then introduce a long and technical order. Neither of them would have time to read it, and over it would go. I got a lot of good legislation for Jackson County over while they shot craps."

CREDIT

Claiming credit for the achievements of the opposition is a political game Harry Truman accused the Republicans of playing.

"With such a record, how in heaven's name can the Republican Party claim credit for the farm program today?" Truman asked a crowd of farmers in Grand Forks, North Dakota, on September 29, 1952. He added: "It reminds me of the flea that was on the back of a donkey crossing a bridge. When they got across, the flea said to the donkey, 'Boy, we sure did shake that bridge, didn't we?' "

CRIMINAL CLASS

"Always, it is the uneducated person, regardless of color, who is the dangerous citizen," Senator Truman warned. "It is the ignorant class among the people that is the criminal class."

(see EDUCATION)

CRISIS

Nearly every crisis seems to be the worst one but after it's over it isn't so bad.

—letter to Martha Truman, August 12, 1945

CRITICS

"I've found that critics are usually picked from frustrated people who have made a failure in the things they criticize," observed President Truman, who, like every president, was criticized by both professional and amateur critics.

"I don't let these things bother me for the simple reason I know that I am trying to do the right thing, and eventually the facts will come out. I'll probably be holding a conference with Saint Peter when that happens."

(see FREEDOM OF EXPRESSION; HUME, PAUL; MUSIC CRITIC)

CUSTER, GENERAL GEORGE

The Douglas MacArthur of his day.
—*Where the Buck Stops* (Margaret Truman, ed.), 1989
(see MACARTHUR, DOUGLAS)

D

DECISIONMAKING

A Chief Executive must be decisive. "If you are going to walk the floor and worry yourself to death every time you have to make a decision," wrote Truman, "or if you fail to make up your mind, then you are not suited for the job."

I have always believed that right will prevail in the end. It has been a policy with me to get the facts and then make a decision. That decision should be made in the public interest as conditions then prevailing require. If the facts available justify a decision at the time it will also be correct in future time.

—*The Autobiography of Harry S. Truman*, 1980

Decisions made by me were made on the facts available. I found that some of them did not work out as anticipated, because of factors unknown at the time the decision was made. I believe in publicly admitting the error and amending the decision. No man can make a perfect score.

—*The Autobiography of Harry S. Truman*, 1980
(see PRESIDENCY)

DE GAULLE, CHARLES

Truman used two words to describe French president Charles de Gaulle:
"A pinhead."

DEGREE

"I have a little hesitation about addressing this august body, shall I say," Truman confessed at a commencement service of the University of California at Berkeley (June 12, 1948), "everybody with degrees emeritus and all the other $40 words that go with an education. The only degree that I ever earned was at George Washington University in Washington, D.C. My daughter went to school there for four years and earned me a degree."

(see COLLEGE)

DEMAGOGUE

Senator Truman was silent in the Senate at first. Asked once by a reporter why he was so reluctant to join the debate, Senator Truman answered, "I'm not going to demagogue until I have something to demagogue about."

DEMAGOGUE-CALLING

Demagogue-calling is a cherished political tradition. Harry Truman, as chairman of the Senate Investigating Committee, intervened once in a demagogue-calling contest between labor leader John L. Lewis and Republican Senator Joseph Ball of Minnesota.

It was unclear which one of the two, Lewis or Ball, had cast the first stone (or called the first "demagogue," as it were) and they were hotly disputing this point when Truman broke it up:

> JOHN L. LEWIS: When you call me a demagogue, I will say you are less than a proper representative of the common people of this country when you do that.
>
> TRUMAN: Now, Mr. Lewis, we don't stand for any sassy remarks to the members of this committee, and your rights will be protected here just the same as those of everybody else. I don't like that remark to a member of this committee.
>
> MR. LEWIS: Senator, did you object when the Senator [Joseph H. Ball] called me a demagogue?
>
> TRUMAN: Yes, it works both ways. I don't think the Senator should have called you a demagogue.
>
> MR. LEWIS: Who cast the first stone?
>
> TRUMAN: I'm stopping it right now.
>
> —transcript, congressional hearings, March 26, 1943
> (see LEWIS, JOHN L.)

DEMOCRACY

"In the battle for men's minds our faith is more appealing, more dynamic, and stronger than any totalitarian force," Truman affirmed at the end of World War II. "The world longs for the kind of tolerance and mutual adjustment which is represented by democratic principles."

Later in life Truman regarded the future: "I am optimistic as I look toward the future, because I believe in the superior attraction for men's minds and hearts of the democratic principles which have been tried and tested in free nations, and which are now winning the allegiance of men throughout the world."

No government is perfect. One of the chief virtues of a democracy, however, is that its defects are always visible and under democratic processes can be pointed out and corrected.

—speech to Congress, March 12, 1947
(see FAITH)

DEMOCRATIC PARTY

"My only objective is to save the Democratic Party," Truman wrote to his friend Charlie Murphy, "as the party of the people, the people who have no pull at the seat of the mighty."

I have never wanted to pose as a prophet, nor do I intend to be one now, but I do want to keep the Democratic party a party of the people. We can never win unless it is.

—letter to Lyndon Baines Johnson, December 11, 1956

DEPRESSION

"Apparently I have offended the Republican gentleman who wants to be president," remarked Truman during the heated 1948 campaign against Thomas Dewey. "Republicans don't like people who talk about depressions. You can hardly blame them for that. You remember the old saying: 'Don't talk about rope in the house where somebody has been hanged.' "

DESCENDANTS

"I do not know whether Presidents ought to have any descendants," Truman commented to students at Columbia

University, "because their descendants inherit the difficult burden of having people expect them to live up to their ancestors."

DEWEY, THOMAS

Harry Truman did not waste praise on his Republican opponent in 1948, nor did he sling mud. He refrained from referring to him by name, generally calling him "my opponent" or "the Republican candidate."

"This year the same candidate is back with us, and he is saying much the same thing: that he likes our Democratic laws, but that he can run them much better than we can.

"It sounds like the same old phonograph record; but this year the record has a crack, and the needle gets stuck in it. The crack was provided by the Republican Eightieth Congress.

"In 1948, every time the candidate says, 'I can do it better,' the crack says, 'We're against it.' "

Truman sometimes poked fun at Dewey, depicting him as an aristocrat, twirling an imaginary mustache, and having "a high-level tea party with the voters."

Truman accused Dewey of "me-tooism," issue-evasion, and chronic vagueness. When Dewey called for unity in a speech, Truman called for clarity: "Of course, we don't know what he means by unity because he won't tell the country where he stands on any of the issues. . . . He doesn't dare tell the country what the real plans of the Republican party are. He's afraid that if he says something, he'll give the whole show away."

Dewey was an overwhelming favorite to win, and was stunned by his defeat. He said later he felt like the man who woke up to find himself inside a coffin with a lily in his hand and thought: "If I'm alive, what am I doing here? And if I'm dead, why do I have to go to the bathroom?"

(see DOCTOR DEWEY, DOUBLE-TALK)

DIET

Margie looked very well except she's too thin. These damned diets the women go for are all wrong. More people die of dieting these days than of eating too much.

—diary, January 3, 1952
(see WEIGHT)

DICTATORSHIP

If you want an efficient government, why then go someplace where they have a dictatorship and you'll get it.

—Columbia University, April 28, 1959
(see COMMUNIST DICTATORSHIP, FAITH, GOVERNMENT)

DIGNITARIES

Dignitaries are much more ideal in print than face to face.

—diary, June 27, 1948

DISAGREE

I'm amazed sometimes when I find that some of you disagree with me. When I consider how you disagree among yourselves, I'm somewhat comforted. I'll begin to think that maybe I'm all right anyway.

—address to American Society of Newspaper Editors, Washington, D.C., April 17, 1948

(see PRESS)

DISNEYLAND

During a trip to California in retirement Bess asked Harry if he would take her to Disneyland. He declined, saying Disneyland was for kids. She promptly asked Charlie Murphy, a friend who was accompanying them, if *he* would take her, and he said he would. The next morning Charlie showed up at their hotel, ready to drive the former first lady to Disneyland. With her was the former president in suit and tie.

"What are you planning for the day, Mr. President?" Charlie asked.

"What do you think I'm planning?" Truman replied. "I'm going to Disneyland!"

DIVERSITY

This American nation of ours is great because of its diversity—because it is a people drawn from many lands and many cultures, bound together by the ideals of human brotherhood. We must remember these things as we go forward in our efforts for world peace.

—commencement address, Howard University, 1952

DOCTOR DEWEY

Truman delivered his famous "Doctor Dewey" parable often during the campaign of 1948:

My opponent is conducting a very peculiar campaign. He has set himself up as a kind of doctor with a magic cure for all the ills of mankind.

Let's imagine that we, the American people, are going to see this doctor. It's just our usual routine checkup which we have every four years.

We go into the doctor's office.

"Doctor," we say, "we're feeling fine."

"Is that so?" asks the doctor. "You been bothered much by issues lately?"

"Not bothered exactly," we say. "Of course, we've had quite a few. We've had the issues of high prices, and housing, education and social security, and a few others."

"That's bad," says the doctor. "You shouldn't have so many issues."

"Is that right?" we say. "We thought that issues were a sign of political health."

"Not at all," says the doctor. "You shouldn't think about issues. What you need is my brand of soothing syrup—I call it 'unity.' "

Then the doctor edges up a little closer.

"Say, you don't look so good," he says.

We say to him, "Well, that seems strange to me, Doc. I never felt stronger, never had more money, and never had a brighter future. What is wrong with me?"

Well, the doctor looks blank, and says, "I never discuss issues with a patient. But what you need is a major operation."

"Will it be serious, Doc?" we say.

"No, not very serious," he says. "It will just mean taking out the complete works and putting in a Republican Administration."

That's the kind of campaign you're getting from the Republicans. They won't talk about the issues, but they insist that a major operation is necessary.

(see DEWEY, THOMAS; DOUBLE-TALK)

DOUBLE-TALK

"This soft talk and double talk," Truman responded to an attack from his rival Thomas Dewey during the 1948 campaign, "this combination of crafty silence and resounding misrepresentation, is an insult to the intelligence of the American voter. It proceeds upon the assumption that you can fool all the people—or enough of them—all the time."

—campaign speech, October 24, 1948
(see DEWEY, THOMAS; DOCTOR DEWEY; LEOPARD)

DREAM

"There is no end to what can be done," President Truman dreamed aloud in his farewell address on January 15, 1953. "I can't help but dream out loud a little here.

"The Tigris and Euphrates Valley can be made to bloom as it did in the times of Babylon and Nineveh. Israel can be made the country of milk and honey as it was in the time of Joshua. There is a plateau in Ethiopia. . . . Enough food can be raised to feed a hundred million people. There are places in South America—places like Colombia and Venezuela and Brazil . . . where food could be raised for millions of people.

"These things can be done, and they are self-liquidating projects. If we can get peace and safety in the world under the United Nations, the developments will come so fast we will not recognize the world in which we now live."

(see FAREWELL ADDRESS)

DUTY

Do your duty, and history will do you justice.

—dedication address for monument to Presidents Jackson, Polk, and Andrew Johnson, Raleigh, N.C., October 19, 1948

E

EARLY

A veteran early-morning riser, Truman gave White House beat reporters a hard time with his early-morning walks. As the yawning correspondents stood in front of Blair House at six in the morning, President Truman strode briskly past, saying, "Stick with me—I haven't started to get up *early* yet."

(see WALKING)

ECONOMIST

"An economist is a man who wears a watch chain with a Phi Beta Kappa key at one end and no watch at the other," Truman liked to say, aware that choosing the right economic advisors could make or break a president.

"Get me a one-handed economist!" Truman exclaimed once. "All my economists say, 'on the one hand, . . . but on on the other hand . . .' "

EDITORS

Editors are peculiar animals—they throw mud and bricks at you the whole year round—then they make one favorable statement which happens to agree with facts and they think they should be hugged and kissed for it.

—memorandum, 1951
(see NEWSPAPER PUBLISHERS, PRESS)

EDUCATED CITIZENSHIP

I have an idea that 100 schools with 1000 students are of much more value to the country than two schools with 50,000 students. The objective is to build character, find brain power and make responsible citizens to keep the freedom of the individual intact. Personal contact with instructors of character is absolutely essential to these objectives. Mass production of college graduates is not the answer to an educated citizenship.

—memorandum, 1953
(see COLLEGE)

EDUCATION

Education is one thing that can't be taken away from you. Nobody can rob you of your education, because that is in your head; that is, if you have any head and are capable of holding it.

—public papers, 1948

People must have freedom of mind for research that makes progress, otherwise there is no use in having an educational system. If everyone remained in the same groove and were taught exactly the same thing, we would end up with a nation of mediocrities.

—*Memoirs, Vol. 2*, 1956

EDUCATION BASICS

The old idea that grammar, rhetoric, logic, arithmetic, geometry, music and astronomy constitute the basis of an education is just as true now as it always has been. Archimedes, Aristotle, Euclid, Galileo, Leonardo da Vinci, Sir Isaac Newton, Einstein all started from these fundamentals, as did the great literary lights and the great musicians.

—memorandum, 1953

EGOTIST

When an egotist is punctured a lot of noise and whistling accompanies the escaping air.

—letter to Edward Thompson, editor of *Life*, January 6, 1956

EISENHOWER, DWIGHT
(U.S. President 1953–1961)

"A decent man, but a bad president." This was Truman's rating of Eisenhower, his successor in the White House. When they met at the White House soon after Eisenhower announced his candidacy, Truman said to him, "Ike, I suggest you go right down to the office of the Republican National Committee and ask them to equip you with an elephant hide about an inch thick. You're going to need it."

As "Ike" prepared to take over the presidency in 1953, Truman remarked privately, "He'll sit here and he'll say, 'Do this! Do that!' and nothing will happen. Poor Ike—it won't be a bit like the Army."

Truman made no secret of his bitter disappointment with Eisenhower's subsequent performance as thirty-fourth president: "I think the ugliest and the dumbest thing that Eisenhower did during his administration, and while he was campaigning before his first term, was the cowardly way he ducked the whole question of McCarthyism even when good, decent people around him were being hurt more and more by that awful and horrible man."

The public Eisenhower was not the real Eisenhower, wrote Truman: "It's interesting that a single thing, that great smile of Eisenhower's, gave him the worldwide and lifelong reputation of being a sunny and amiable man, when those of us who knew him well were all too well aware that he was essentially a surly, angry, and disagreeable man."

Truman's main criticism of Eisenhower was not what Ike did but what Ike did not do: "Eisenhower really didn't *do* anything or *decide* anything. He passed the buck, down. . . .

"Nonaction was characteristic of Eisenhower as president because he proved to be such a dumb son of a bitch when he got out of his uniform. . . .

"He is not as intelligent as I thought. Evidently his staff has furnished the intelligence."

I didn't say I was for him, because I knew he didn't know what he was, Democrat or Republican; and he doesn't yet.
— remarks, Columbia University, April 28, 1959

I never had any falling out with him. The only trouble was, he had a lot of damn fool Republicans around him. He's a good man.

— comment, December 1963
(see ANCESTORS, BRASS HALO, IKE)

ENEMIES

"There is no conversation so sweet as that of former political enemies," Truman reflected in retirement. "The way I look at it, I have been blessed in both enemies and friends."

ENGLAND

During a visit to England in 1956, Truman was asked how he was getting along in the old country. So far, he replied, he had not needed an interpreter.

"A good many of the difficulties between our two countries spring not from our differences but from the fact we are so much alike," Truman told reporters. "Another problem we have is that in election years we behave somewhat as primitive peoples do at the time of the full moon."

EPITAPH

Truman liked to quote an epitaph from a Tombstone, Arizona, cemetery that said, "Here lies Jack Williams. He done his damnedest."

"I think that is the greatest epitaph a man can have, when he gives everything that is in him to the job he had before him. That is all you can ask of him and that is what I have tried to do."

F

FACTS

I thought, perhaps, you might be interested in the facts.
—letter to Richmond, Virginia, *Times-Dispatch*, July 9, 1947
(disputing a report that appeared in the paper)

FAIR PRICES

The Republicans will be happy to see fair prices, if prices happen to be fair. If they don't happen to be fair, well, prosperity is just around the corner.
—Grand Forks, North Dakota, September 29, 1952
(see PROSPERITY, REPUBLICANS)

FAITH

Efficiency alone is not enough in government. . . . Hitler learned that efficiency without justice is a vain thing. Democracy does not work that way. Democracy is a matter of faith—a faith in the soul of man—a faith in human rights. . . . Faith is much more than efficiency. Faith gives value to all things. Without faith, the people perish.

—St. Paul, Minnesota, October 13, 1948

(see DEMOCRACY)

FAREWELL ADDRESS

In President Truman's farewell address of January 15, 1953, he reminded Americans that "the great issues remain the same . . ."

The Communists cannot deprive us of our liberties—fear can. The Communists cannot stamp out our faith in human dignity—fear can. Fear is an enemy within ourselves; and, if we do not root it out, it may destroy the very way of life we are so anxious to protect.

To beat back fear, we must hold fast to our heritage as free men. We must renew our confidence in one another, our tolerance, our sense of being neighbors, fellow citizens. We must take our stand on the Bill of Rights. The inquisition, the star chamber, have no place in a free society.

Our ultimate strength lies not alone in arms, but in the sense of moral values and moral truths that give meaning and vitality to the purposes of free people. These values are our faith, our inspiration, the source of our strength, and our indomitable determination.

We face hard tasks, great dangers. But we are Americans and we have faced hardships and uncertainty before; we have adjusted before to changing circumstances. Our whole history has been a steady training for the work it is now ours to do.

No one can lose heart for the task, none can lose faith in our free ways, who stops to remember where we began, what we have sought, and what accomplished, all together as Americans. . . .

Let all of us pause now, think back, consider carefully the meaning of our national experience. Let us draw comfort from it and faith and confidence in our future as Americans.

The Nation's business is never finished. The basic questions we have been dealing with, these eight years past, present themselves anew. That is the way of our society. Circumstances change and current questions take on different forms, new complications, year by year. But underneath, the great issues remain the same—prosperity, welfare, human rights, effective democracy, and above all, peace.

FARMING

Harry Truman wanted to go to college after high school, but family responsibilities prevented it. Instead, he spent the next ten years managing his family's six-hundred-acre farm.

He later called his years on the farm "the best ten years of my life."

Farming was good training for a future leader. "I thought of Cincinnatus and a lot of other farm boys who had made good, and I thought maybe by cussing mules and plowing corn I could perhaps overcome my shyness and amount to something."

FATHER

When a reporter asked about Truman's father, John Anderson Truman, referring to him as a "failure," Harry Truman interrupted testily: "How could my father be called a failure? After all, he was the father of a President of the United States."

FBI

"We want no Gestapo or Secret Police," President Truman wrote in his diary on May 12, 1945, during his first month in office. "F.B.I. is tending in that direction. They are dabbling in sex life scandals and plain blackmail when they should be catching criminals. . . . *This must stop.*"

FEELING

"How do you feel, Mr. President?" President Truman was asked by a reporter. It was not the first time Truman had been asked this question.

"If I felt any better," he replied, "I couldn't stand it."

FINE PRINT

Thick eyeglasses earned young Harry Truman taunts from other boys in school. They called him "Four Eyes" and "Bookworm." But it was worth it to be able to see clearly. "When I first put the glasses on," Truman recollected, "I saw things and saw print I'd never seen before. I learned to read when I was five but never could see the fine print." He added: "I've been 'fine printed' many a time since I've been able to read it."

FLYING SAUCERS

"Mr. President, have you seen any flying saucers?"

The question was asked at the president's news conference of July 10, 1947, soon after a reported "flying disk" crash near Roswell, New Mexico.

Truman replied laconically, "Only in the newspapers."

FOREIGN POLICY

"Mr. President," a reporter called out, "the New York Times this morning has a story out of Paris saying that there is— may be—a drastic change in our foreign policy. . . ."

"I haven't heard about it," snapped Truman, "and I make the policy."

Our foreign policy was mistakenly called by some a policy of containment. This is not true. Our purpose was much broader. We were working for a united, free and prosperous world.

—*Memoirs*, Vol. 2, 1956

FREEDOM HOUSE AWARD

"You don't know how overcome I am," said Truman upon receiving the Freedom House award in New York City in April 1965, after a praise-packed introduction. "You don't know how difficult it is to be present at your own funeral and still able to walk around."

FREEDOM OF EXPRESSION

In a free country, we punish men for the crimes they commit, but never for the opinions they have. And the reason this is so fundamental to freedom is not, as many suppose, that it protects the few unorthodox from suppression by the majority. To permit freedom of expression is primarily for the benefit of the majority because it protects criticism, and criticism leads to progress. . . . We need not fear the expression of ideas—we do need to fear their suppression.

—on his presidential veto of Internal Security Act, 1950

FRIEND

A small funeral took place in Independence, Missouri, in February 1966. At first only the undertaker and the minister stood by the casket. At the burial time announced in the newspaper a distinguished older gentleman pulled up in a green Chrysler. Eighty-three years old, frail, in poor health, Harry Truman hobbled up to the bier and braved the bitter cold to stand by it through the entire ceremony.

After it was over, the minister asked Truman why he put himself through such an ordeal.

"Pastor," Truman answered, "I never forget a friend."

FRONT PORCH

The first day at sea on the ship [U.S.S.] *Augusta* sailing to the Potsdam meeting, the President excused himself and told his staff he wanted to "go out on the front porch for a while."

Teased later about his use of the not very nautical term "front porch," Truman replied:

"The only time I was at sea before was going to France and back in the last war. Now, wouldn't it be silly for me to ape the language of men whose business is ships?"

FULBRIGHT, WILLIAM

An overeducated s.o.b.

— description of the senator after the Fulbright Committee report, "Favoritism and Influence," was released on February 5, 1951

FUTURE

Harry Truman charged his Republican rival Thomas Dewey with being vague about the issues.

"In a prepared speech delivered in Phoenix, Arizona, the Republican candidate solemnly informed the people at Phoenix, and I quote, 'You know that your future is still ahead of you.' Exciting, don't you think?

"I was greatly impressed by this bold stand of the Republican candidate. . . .

"At last I found an issue on which he was willing to take a position. . . . He's for the future.

"But this position did remind me of a little verse . . . we learned as school children . . . which goes something like this:

> "There is nothing here but the present
> Nothing behind but the past,
> Nothing ahead but the future,
> My Gosh, how long will it last?"

G

GARAGE SLOGANS

Herbert Hoover once ran on the slogan, "Two cars in every garage." Apparently the Republican candidate this year is running on the slogan, "Two families in every garage."

—campaign speech, Chicago Stadium, October 1948
(see REPUBLICANS)

GENERALS

All through history it's the nations that have given the most to the generals and the least to the people that have been the first to fall.

—quoted by Merle Miller in *Plain Speaking*, 1973
(see MACARTHUR, DOUGLAS)

GENERATION

"Our American political situation is about the same from generation to generation," Truman reflected on the lessons of history. "The main difficulty is that the rising generation never knows about the acts of the previous one—most people think it is too much trouble to find out."

(see HISTORY)

GETTING ALONG

In his youth Truman was not much of a rebel; he was more of a people pleaser, and not the first to learn that getting along led to getting ahead.

"I used to watch my father and mother closely to learn what I could do to please them," he wrote in his *Memoirs* (1955), "just as I did with my schoolteachers and playmates. Because of my efforts to get along with my associates I usually was able to get what I wanted."

GHOSTS

The White House is haunted, according to legend. President Truman upheld the ghostly tradition in a letter to his wife on June 12, 1945:

> I sit here in this old house and work on foreign affairs, read reports, and work on speeches—all the while listening to the ghosts walk up and down the hallway and even right here in the study.
> The floors pop and the drapes move back and forth—I can just imagine old Andy and Teddy having an argument over Franklin. Or James Buchanan and Franklin Pierce deciding which was the more useless to the country. And when Millard Fillmore and Chester Arthur join in for place and show the din is almost unbearable. But I still get some work done. . . .

In September of the following year Truman wrote his wife that he was awakened in the middle of the night by a distinct knock on his bedroom door: "This old place

53

cracks and pops all night long and you can very well imagine that old Jackson or Andy Johnson or some other ghost is walking. Why they'd want to come back here I could never understand."

Later President Truman was asked about ghosts by an interviewer.

"Now about these ghosts," he replied. "I'm sure they're here and I'm not half so alarmed at meeting up with any of them as I am at having to meet the live nuts I have to see every day."

(see CRACKPOTS, NUTS)

GLASSES

A Kansas City eye doctor prescribed thick glasses for young Harry Truman and warned him to avoid football, baseball, or any other popular sports or activities, so the glasses would not get broken. This separated Truman from his peers and forced him to take refuge in the world of books during his formative years.

"I've worn glasses since I was six years old," Truman told Merle Miller, "and of course, they called me *four-eyes* and a lot of other things, too.That's hard on a boy. It makes him lonely, and it gives him an inferiority complex, and he has a hard time overcoming it. . . . But you can overcome it. You've got to fight for everything you do. You've got to be above those calling you names, and you've got to do more work than they do, but it usually comes out all right in the end."

Harry Truman almost lost his glasses—and his life— one night during World War I. Captain Truman was riding his horse Dobbin in advance of his men to study the German lines and phone firing instructions back to Battery D. As he rode under a low-hanging tree, his glasses were knocked off by a branch. There was no time to find a spare pair. Legally blind in one eye, Truman could scarcely see anything in the darkness without his glasses.

"There he was in the middle of the biggest battle in the history of the world, practically blind," Margaret Truman described it. "He turned around, frantically trying to catch a glimpse of the glasses on the road. A glint of light on the horse's back—dawn was just beginning to break—caught his eye. There were the glasses, sitting on Dobbin's rump."

(see BIOGRAPHY 1918)

GOD

I never thought God picked any favorites. It is my studied opinion that any race, creed or color can be God's favorites if they act the part and very few of them do that.

—diary, June 1, 1945

I've never thought that God gives a damn about pomp and circumstance, gold crowns, jeweled breast plates and ancestral background.

—diary, St. Louis, February 2, 1955
(see CHURCH, JESUS, PRAYER, RELIGION)

GOD'S TIME

"Bess and Margaret went to Missouri at 7:30 EDT, 6:30 God's time," President Truman wrote in his diary on July 19, 1948, after his wife and daughter returned to Independence. "I sure hated to see them go."

GOLF

Truman had only one complaint about golf, he said: "I never had enough money to play golf."

GOVERNMENT

"The Government will build the power dams," candidate Dwight Eisenhower spoke sarcastically as he campaigned against "Big Government" in 1952. "The Government will do this and that, the Government does everything but come in and wash the dishes for the housewife."

When President Truman read this statement by Ike he commented: "I'm not sure what the accusation is, whether it is that we built the dams or that we didn't wash the dishes."

Truman added: "Half the fun of being a citizen in this country comes from complaining about the way we run our government—state, federal, and local."

He denied being for Big Government. "The least government is the best government," he asserted. "We should have just as little as we can get along with."

I think we have the greatest government the world has ever seen. The more I become familiar with it, the better I like it, even if it does make a slave out of the President.

—press conference, May 9, 1947

I think our Constitution and its Bill of Rights is the greatest document of government in the history of the world and I am doing my best to contribute my share to upholding it.

—memorandum, 1950

It has always been my opinion that those who profit most from government expenditures should pay most for the support of the government.

—memorandum, 1950

Once a government is committed to the principle of silencing the voice of opposition, it has only one way to go, and that is down the path of increasingly repressive measures, until it becomes a source of terror to all its citizens and creates a country where everyone lives in fear.

—remarks, August 8, 1950
(see DICTATORSHIP)

GRAND COULEE DAM

"This dam had to be fought for!" declared Truman at the opening of the Grand Coulee Dam in Grand Coulee, Washington, on May 11, 1950. "You remember what its opponents said . . . 'Up in the Grand Coulee country there is no one to sell power to except the coyotes and jackrabbits and there never will be.' . . . Today, those who opposed Grand Coulee are trying to cover their tracks. . . . But they can't erase the record. They did not understand then, and they do not understand now . . . that the United States is a growing dynamic country. They saw no need to plan and work for a greater future. The way things were was good enough for them."

(see ACORN THINKING, DREAM)

GRANT, ULYSSES
(U.S. President 1869–1877)

"The worst president in our history."

Such was Truman's harsh assessment of Ulysses Grant, the eighteenth president. He admired Grant as a general:

"He said what you have to do to fight a war, you have to find the enemy, and you have to hit him with everything you've got, and then you've got to keep right on going. And that's what he did. He never stopped to issue fancy statements about this and that. He just kept right on going."

But as a president Truman found fault with Grant:

"Grant was typical of the soldier-president. Without any understanding of political machinery, he was able to ride

57

into office on the popularity which military victory always brings. . . .

"He wasn't even a chief executive; he was another sleepwalker whose administration was even more crooked than Warren Harding's, if that's possible. . . . After he got elected in 1868, why the people around him were stealing the country blind.

"Grant had the idea that Congress was supposed to run things, and he thought being President was just sort of . . . like that other fella we've discussed [Eisenhower], some kind of ceremonial job where all you had to do was entertain visiting royalty and pin medals on people and shake hands and getting your picture taken with a big grin on your face."

(see EISENHOWER, DWIGHT; MILITARY LEADERS)

GREATNESS

In a memorandum written on May 14, 1932, hours before announcing his candidacy for the Senate, Harry Truman wrote: "In reading the lives of great men, I found that the first victory they won was over themselves . . . self-discipline with all of them came first. I found that most of the really great ones never thought they were great."

Later asked by biographer William Hillman if in his boyhood he dreamed of being president, Truman said no. "I studied the lives of great men and famous women; and I found that the men and women who got to the top were those who did the jobs they had in hand, with everything they had of energy and enthusiasm and hard work. I had no idea the lightning would ever strike me, as it has."

Truman was more concerned with being right than being great. "Well, all the great—those we call great—like Alexander and Caesar and Napoleon, and those pretenders to greatness, like Hitler and Mussolini and Lenin—base their powers on war and the results of war."

In the picture of the great in the United States, most were honorable, hardworking men who were ready when opportunity knocked. Most had training on the farm, in finance or in the military. Well, I tried all three!
—*The Autobiography of Harry S. Truman*, 1980
(see also JOB, MILITARY LEADERS, PRESIDENTS)

GROCERY PRICES

"Mr. President, have you given any thought to grocery prices?" a reporter asked.

"I have given it no thought," admitted the President, "only when I go to pay my bill."

GUESS

Truman did not like guesswork and often refused to guess when asked speculative questions by reporters. "I can't tell you now," he snapped back to a reporter at a press conference on October 17, 1947. "I can't operate on 'by guess or by God.' "

H

⚜

HAPPINESS

Happiness is a state of mind. A farmhand, if he has an ample living, can be just as happy as a millionaire with homes in Maine and Florida. Wealth is a relative proposition, but all . . . must be assured of an opportunity to work and then it's up to them.

—*Mr. President*, 1960

HARD HEAD

"And I congratulate you on the ribbons I see here before me," President Truman said at a National Guard award ceremony on October 26, 1950, in Washington, D.C.

"I wish I could sport some of them. I pinned a medal on General MacArthur the other day, and told him I wished I had a medal like that, and he said that it was my duty to give the medals not receive them. That is always the way. About all I receive is the bricks. It's a good thing I have got a pretty hard head or it would have been broken a long time ago."

(see AWARD; MACARTHUR, DOUGLAS)

HARDING, WARREN G.
(U.S. President 1921–1923)

Alice Roosevelt Longworth . . . once said about him, "Harding was not a bad man. He was just a slob." I think she was being entirely too kind.

—Where the Buck Stops (Margaret Truman, ed.), 1989

HARRISON, BENJAMIN
(U.S. President 1889–1893)

I tend to pair up Benjamin Harrison and Dwight Eisenhower because they're the two presidents I can think of who most preferred laziness to labor.

—Where the Buck Stops (Margaret Truman, ed.), 1989
(see EISENHOWER, DWIGHT)

HEALTH INSURANCE

"I have had some bitter disappointments as President," reflected Truman in retirement, "but the one that has troubled me most, in a personal way, has been the failure to defeat organized opposition to a national compulsory health insurance program."

Truman's Fair Deal proposal for national health insurance was branded "socialized medicine" by the American Medical Association's physicians, who financed a massive lobbying campaign against it.

"When I was on the County Court in Jackson County I saw many a patient refused entrance to a hospital because he didn't have the right physician," Truman wrote in a letter in 1949.

"I am trying to fix it so the people in the middle income bracket can live as long as the very rich and the very poor."

(see also NATIONAL HEALTH, SOCIALISM)

HEAT

One of the results of this system is that it gives the president a good many hot potatoes to handle—but the president gets a lot of hot potatoes from every direction anyhow, and a man who can't handle them has no business in that job. That makes me think of a saying that I used to hear from my old friend and colleague on the Jackson County Court. He said, "Harry, if you can't stand the heat you better get out of the kitchen."

—Wright Memorial Dinner, Washington, D.C., December 17, 1952

HEAVEN

When the gates of Heaven are reached by the shades of the earth bound, the rank and riches enjoyed on this planet won't be of value. Some of our grandees will have to do a lot of explaining on how they got that way. Wish I could hear their alibis! I can't for the probabilities are I'll be thinking up some for myself.

—diary, St. Louis, February 2, 1955

HELL

"Give 'em hell, Harry!"

Truman gave this explanation of the origin of the famous phrase that became the battle cry of his 1948 presidential campaign:

"Well, that started out in the Northwest, in Seattle, Washington. It was in 1948, and we were holding an enthusiastic meeting there when some man with a great big voice cried out from the galleries, 'Give 'em hell, Harry!'

"I told him at that time, and I have been repeating it ever since, that I have never deliberately given anybody hell. I just tell the truth on the opposition—and they think it's hell."

"Give-'em-hell Harry" did not believe in giving them hell at home as well as at work. According to his son-in-law, Clifton Daniel, "Give-'em-hell Harry didn't give anybody hell at home."

Nor did Truman believe in giving the opposition hell after they were defeated. On the day after his stunning upset victory in 1948 the winner announced, graciously, "I am through giving them hell."

There was a story, almost certainly apocryphal, that after the birth of his first grandchild, Harry Truman told his daughter Margaret, "When he gets older, I'm going to teach him to talk."

And Margaret replied, "The hell you are."

From now on I'm going to do as I please and let 'em all go to hell.

—letter to his mother and sister, November 18, 1946

HERO

"All the people, no matter where they come from, like a winner, like a hero," President Truman noted. "You have no doubt been at a ballgame when the shortstop would make a home run in an early inning and fail to catch one out in the field later. He is a hero the first time, and they throw pop bottles at him the second time. He needs sympathy in both instances, but seldom gets it, so I never pay any attention to bricks which are thrown my way or to compliments which come my way."

HIDING

"Hiding" was something Truman did *to* the opposition, not *from* it. "I hope you will listen to my speech tonight," he told a crowd in Akron on October 11, 1948. He vowed: "I'm going to take the hide off 'em from top to bottom. I hate to have to do that, but they have it coming."

HIGH HEELS

President Truman invited his daughter Margaret to join him on an early morning walk. It would give them an opportunity to talk, he said persuasively.

She agreed to go along the next day. In her biography of her father, *Harry Truman* (1973), Margaret described what happened.

"The President sets out from White House at his usual 120 strides a minute. He pauses at the corner to find out why daughter is thirty feet behind him. 'Come on, Margie,' he says, 'what's holding you up?'

" 'Where's the fire?' asks his gasping daughter. Two more blocks at 120 paces per minute and the President pauses again. His daughter is now sixty feet behind him. 'What's the matter with you anyway?' he asks impatiently.

" 'I'm wearing high heels,' explains daughter weakly.

" 'Why don't you buy some sensible shoes?'

"End of father-daughter chats on morning walks."

(see WALKING)

HISTORY

"There is nothing new in the world," Truman liked to say, "except the history you do not know."

As a boy he read *Heroes of History* and many other historical biographies and concluded, "Men make history, history does not make the man."

It was an opinion he never changed, even after he changed history and history changed him.

"My debt to history is one which cannot be calculated," he wrote in his *Memoirs*. "I know of no other motivation which so accounts for my awakening interest as a young lad in the principles of leadership and government. . . .

"Reading history, to me, was far more than a romantic adventure. It was solid instruction and wise teaching which I somehow felt that I wanted and needed. . . .

"While still a boy I could see that history had some extremely valuable lessons to teach. I learned from it that a leader is a man who has the ability to get other people to do what they don't want to do, and like it."

Truman was a voracious reader of history and, though his formal education was limited, probably knew as much history as any president.

"History taught me that the leader of any country, in order to assume his responsibilities as a leader, must know the history of not only his own country but of all the other great countries, and that he must make the effort to apply this knowledge. . . .

"You must know the historical background of what makes the worlds go 'round. After all, there is little real change in the problems of government from the beginnings of time down to the present."

Learning history is preparation for making history, Truman told his biographer William Hillman. "I'm a great optimist about people and their future. But it's not enough to know history without doing something about the future. . . .

"History is a story of improvement even if there are setbacks. Since the Renaissance there has been a constant improvement. But another world war would put civilization back some thousand years or more."

Truman felt we can learn from history to avoid repeating

the mistakes of the past, including the mistake often repeated by leaders, of not knowing when to stop.

Of Caesar, Truman said: "His big trouble was that he didn't know when to stop. Alexander suffered from the same thing, and you'll find men like that all through history, most recently, of course, Hitler, and if we'd let him get away with it, Stalin had the same thing in mind. . . .

"To hell with them . . . When history is written they will be the sons of bitches—not I."

When I was young . . . I read everything I could get my hands on about men who made history. The simplest conclusion I reached was that the lazy men caused all the trouble and those who worked had the job of rectifying their mistakes.

—letter to Minnesota governor Orville Freeman, February 7, 1958

I was an avid reader of history and particularly the lives of great men and famous women. I found that some were born to greatness, some attained it by accident, and some worked for it.

—*The Autobiography of Harry S. Truman*, 1980

It is not possible for a public man to be constantly worrying about what history and future generations will say about decisions he has to make. He must live in the present, do what he thinks is right at the time, and history will take care of itself.

—*The Autobiography of Harry S. Truman*, 1980

Throughout history, those who have tried hardest to do the right thing have often been persecuted, misrepresented, or even assassinated, but eventually what they stood for has come to the top and been adopted by the people.

—*Memoirs, Vol. 2*, 1956

HOBBY

Asked what his favorite hobby was, Truman adamantly denied having a hobby. He declared, "I've never had a hobby in my life."

HONESTY

"I have always believed in Santa Claus I guess," Harry Truman wrote in a diary entry in 1931 after losing an argument with his wife Bess over the honesty of the human race.

" 'The Boss' says that instead of most being honest most of them are not when they are put into a position where they can get away with crookedness. I guess I've been wrong in my premise that 92% are ethically honest. Maybe 92% are not thieves but it is a certainty that 92% are not ethically honest."

I can always get along with an honest man.
> —quoted by Margaret Truman in *Harry S. Truman*, 1973

HONOR

Good name and honor are worth more than all the gold and jewels ever mined.
> —quoted by Margaret Truman in *Harry S. Truman*, 1973
> (see also REWARD)

HOOVER, HERBERT
(U.S. President 1929–1933)

When his opponent, Thomas Dewey, called him a "bureaucrat," Truman called Dewey a "Hoovercrat"—a reference to Herbert Hoover, the Depression-plagued thirty-first president.

"You remember the Hoover cart—the remains of the old

Tin Lizzie being pulled by a mule because you couldn't afford to buy a new car or gas for the old one. First you had the Hoovercrats and then you had the Hoover carts. One always follows the other."

When former president Hoover came to Washington, D.C., years later, President Truman put partisan politics aside and called him at his hotel to invite him over.

Hoover, who had not visited the White House since FDR's election, said he would be happy to come over.

"Well," Truman chuckled, "I took the liberty of anticipating you. I already have a car on the way over to your hotel to bring you."

President Truman was very cordial to Hoover, and during his second term he did the unthinkable—he asked the former Republican president for advice. Truman appointed Hoover to do a study and make recommendations for the reorganization of the executive branch. Hoover was grateful to Truman for the recognition, saying, "Mr. President, I think you have added ten years to my life by giving me this job."

HORSE MANURE

President Truman was often criticized for his hot language.

One day at a press conference the president called someone's comment a "bunch of horse manure."

When this was reported back to the First Lady, she was not surprised. Bess smiled and said, "You don't know how many years it took me to tone it down to that."

(see S.O.B.)

HORSE RACES

You people know a great deal about horse races in Lexington, and you know it doesn't matter which horse is ahead or behind at any given moment, it's the horse that comes out ahead at the finish that counts.

—Lexington, Kentucky, October 1, 1948
(see POLLS)

HORSE'S MOUTH

During a campaign stop in Ardmore, Oklahoma, the candidate expressed admiration for a cowboy's palamino horse. Truman stopped, opened the horse's mouth, examined it, and pronounced the horse to be six years old.

"Correct!" exclaimed the cowboy.

The story appeared in newspapers across the country with the headline: TRUMAN GETS RIGHT DOPE FROM THE HORSE'S MOUTH.

HUMAN

"Haven't you ever been overawed by a secretary?" asked Truman, who was himself very human, "and finally, when you have reached the man you wanted to see, discovered he was very human?"

HUMAN ANIMAL

The human animal and his emotions change not much from age to age. He must change now or he faces absolute and complete destruction and maybe the insect age or an atmosphereless planet will succeed him.

—memorandum, dated only "1946"

HUMAN NATURE

"There's nothing new in human nature," Harry Truman noted, "only our names for things change."

(see HISTORY)

HUMANITY

"More than half the people of the world are living in conditions approaching misery," observed President Truman. "For the first time in history humanity possesses the knowledge and the skill to relieve the suffering of these people."

There are those who have said that this is America's century, but we want it to be more than that. We want it to be humanity's century.

—commencement address, Howard University, 1952

HUME, PAUL

Margaret Truman gave a concert at Constitution Hall in Washington in December 1950. Paul Hume, music critic for the *Washington Post*, angered Harry Truman with such critical comments as, "She is flat a good deal of the time," "She cannot sing with anything approaching professional finish," and "She communicates almost nothing of the music she presents."

President Truman wrote this note to Paul Hume, never expecting Hume to publish it:

> I have just read your lousy review buried in the back pages. You sound like a frustrated man that never made a success, an eight-ulcer man on a four-ulcer job, and all four ulcers working.
>
> I never met you, but if I do you'll need a new nose and plenty of beefsteak and perhaps a supporter below. Westbrook Pegler, a guttersnipe, is a gentleman compared to you. You can take that as more of an insult than a reflection on your ancestry.

Hume went public with the letter, which proved to be an embarrassment to the president. Hume himself, however, was more sympathetic. He was aware that the president's close friend and press secretary Charlie Ross had just died. Hume wrote, "I can only say that a man suffering the loss of a friend and carrying the burden of the present world crisis ought to be indulged in an occasional outburst of temper."

Eight years later Paul Hume visited the Truman Library and asked to see the ex-president.

Truman laughed when he heard Hume's name announced. Truman gave Hume a tour of the library and spent an hour entertaining his ex-nemesis, to whom he said: "I've had a lot of fun with you and General MacArthur over the years. I hope you don't mind."

(see also CRITICS; MACARTHUR, DOUGLAS; MUSIC CRITIC)

HUMOR

"While intolerance is running rampant throughout the world, we need more friendly people, like those who grew so naturally out of the mind of Mark Twain, that kindly humorist from Hannibal, to guide us back to basic principles," said Vice President Truman in the Missouri capital of Jefferson City on February 22, 1945. "No matter how grave the postwar problems may be, I am sure that our American sense of proportion and—yes—our sense of humor, will see us through to victory."

(see TWAIN, MARK)

HUNTING

Truman declined an invitation to join a hunting party with this terse explanation: "I do not like to hunt animals, and I never have. I don't like to shoot at anything that can't shoot back."

I

IDEALIST

"Went into business all enthusiastic," Truman wrote in his diary in 1930, jotting down the short version of his life story so far.

"Lost all I had and all I could borrow. Mike Pendergast picked me up and put me into politics and I've been lucky. I'm still an idealist and I still believe that Jehovah will reward the righteous and punish the wrongdoers . . ."

(see POLITICS, RIGHT)

IDEAS

Men with ideas can express those ideas only where there is freedom of education.

—Memoirs, Vol. 2, 1956
(see EDUCATION)

IKE

Making a campaign speech for Adlai Stevenson in We-
natchee, Washington, in the fall of 1952, President Truman
noticed a boy with an I LIKE IKE sign.

"Now I see a kid back there who had been paid to carry
that 'I like Ike' sign. Well, I like Ike—I like Ike so well that
I would send him back to the Army, if I had the chance.
And that's what I'm trying to do."

(see ANCESTORS; EISENHOWER, DWIGHT)

IMPUDENCE

If they want to ask me some impudent questions, I'll try to
give them some impudent answers.

—at a Columbia University lecture, April 27, 1959

INAUGURAL ADDRESS

"Weather permitting, I hope to be present," Truman wrote
in a coy response to an official invitation to his inauguration.

The Truman Inaugural Address of January 20, 1949, is
remembered for its stirring defense of democracy and
clear definition of the differences between communism
and democracy.

> Communism is based on the belief that man is so weak
> and inadequate that he is unable to govern himself, and
> therefore requires the rule of strong masters.
>
> Democracy is based on the conviction that man has the
> moral and intellectual capacity, as well as the inalienable
> right, to govern himself with reason and justice.
>
> Communism subjects the individual to arrest without
> lawful cause, punishment without trial, and forced labor
> as the chattel of the state. It decrees what information he
> shall receive, what art he shall produce, what leaders he
> shall follow, and what thoughts he shall think.

Democracy maintains that government is established for the benefit of the individual, and is charged with the responsibility of protecting the rights of the individual and his freedom in the exercise of his abilities.

Communism maintains that social wrongs can be corrected only by violence.

Democracy has proved that social justice can be achieved through peaceful change.

Communism holds that the world is so deeply divided into opposing classes that war is inevitable.

Democracy holds that free nations can settle differences justly and maintain lasting peace.

These differences between communism and democracy do not concern the United States alone. People everywhere are coming to realize that what is involved is material well-being, human dignity, and the right to believe in and worship God.

I state these differences, not to draw issues of belief as such, but because the actions resulting from the Communist philosophy are a threat to the efforts of free nations to bring about a world recovery and lasting peace.

Since the end of hostilities, the United States has invested its substance and its energy in a great constructive effort to restore peace, stability, and freedom in the world. . . .

Democracy alone can supply the vitalizing force to stir the peoples of the world into triumphant action, not only against their human oppression, but also against their ancient enemies—hunger, misery, and despair.

If we are to be successful in carrying out these policies, it is clear that we must have continued prosperity in this country and we must keep ourselves strong.

Slowly but surely we are weaving a world fabric of international security and growing prosperity.

We are aided by all who want relief from the lies of propaganda—who desire truth and sincerity.

We are aided by all who long for economic security—for the security and abundance that men in free societies can enjoy.

We are aided by all who desire freedom of speech, freedom of religion, and freedom to live their own lives for useful ends. . . .

We are aided by all who wish to live in freedom from fear. . . .

I say to all men, what we have achieved in liberty we will surpass in greater liberty.

Steadfast in our faith in the Almighty, we will advance toward a world where man's freedom is secure.

To that end we will devote our strength, our resources, and our firmness of resolve. With God's help, the future of mankind will be assured in a world of justice, harmony, and peace.

(see COMMUNISM, DEMOCRACY)

INDEPENDENCE, MISSOURI

The most famous resident of Independence, Missouri, returned home on November 1, 1948, at the end of his "give-'em-hell" presidential campaign. The press plane landed at the airport after the President had already started off by car for home. The reporters and photographers rushed after him in press cars and raced to reach his home ahead of him. When he arrived a few minutes later, a reporter asked him why he was late.

"Oh, we were stopped by a police car and had to pull over," answered Truman. "Seems there were some very important people going through town."

After leaving office on January 20, 1953, Harry Truman returned home to live his remaining years in Independence. "I've had every political office, nearly, from precinct to president of the United States," he said, "and I came back home to live at the end of it all."

INDIVIDUALISM

In the race for the Senate in 1934, Truman's opponent, Senator Patterson, was a self-proclaimed "rugged individualist." Truman explained to the people what that meant:

"Now, rugged individualism means ... allowing no consideration of the rights of nonrugged individuals to stand in the way of success. Happily for us at this time, we have few rugged individualists left aside from Senator Patterson."

INTERNATIONAL LAW

When Kansas and Colorado have a quarrel over the water in the Arkansas River they don't call out the National Guard in each state and go to war over it. They bring a suit in the Supreme Court of the United States and abide by the decision. There isn't a reason in the world why we cannot do that internationally.

—Kansas City, Missouri, April, 1945

ISRAEL

Under instruction from President Truman, the United States officially recognized the state of Israel eleven minutes after its midnight proclamation of May 15, 1948.

"God put you in your mother's womb," Chief Rabbi of Israel Isaac Halevi Herzog said to President Truman when they met at the White House, "so you would be the instrument to bring about the rebirth of Israel after two thousand years."

This remark brought rare tears to Truman's eyes.

ISSUE

When you want to confuse an issue always talk about what it will do to something that has no relation to it.

—*The Autobiography of Harry S. Truman*, 1980

J

JACKSON, ANDREW
(U.S. President 1829–1837)

Truman rated Andrew Jackson, the seventh president, among the greatest of the presidential gallery.

"It takes courage to face a duelist with a pistol and it takes courage to face a British general with an army. But it takes still greater and far higher courage to face friends with a grievance. The bravest thing Andrew Jackson ever did was stand up and tell his own people to their faces that they were wrong."

Truman took inspiration from Jackson: "One thing I always liked about Jackson was that he brought the basic issues into clear focus. People knew what he stood for and what he was against. . . .

"He represented the man with a hole in his pocket just as much as he represented the big shots."

JEFFERSON, THOMAS
(U.S. President 1801–1809)

Truman rated Thomas Jefferson as second only to George Washington in his personal list of the greatest presidents. He considered himself a "modern Jeffersonian," one who lived in an industrial rather than an agrarian society.

"The Adamses and the New England historians made a crook and atheist out of Thomas Jefferson," wrote Truman, "until honest research proved 'em in error (to put it mildly)."

While many historians discounted the story (already part of African-American folklore), that "slave-mistress" Sally Hemmings bore Thomas Jefferson five children, Truman believed it was true.

"The thing that's certain, in any case, is that, for some of the time Jefferson was in France, Sally was there, too, and took care of Jefferson's daughter Polly, and that the love affair with Sally lasted thirty-eight years."

The relationship with Sally Hemmings did not seem to diminish Jefferson's stature in Truman's view, nor did the contemporary image of Jefferson as an "egghead."

"I suppose the people today who use the word 'egghead' as a pejorative term . . . would call him one; but if he was an egghead, he was a practical egghead. He knew how to make things work on the ground as well as to read and talk about them. His particular talent was understanding free government and how it can be made to work, and I think that was the most outstanding contribution that Jefferson made to the history of the United States.

"If you want to call a man an egghead who has a knowledge of all sorts of things, who's well versed in history and everything else, and who's also a practical politician and can make good government work, then he certainly was an egghead."

(see ADAMS, JOHN; NEWSPAPER PUBLISHERS)

JESUS

A couple of golden crowns with all kinds of expensive jewels have been stolen from a Roman Catholic shrine in Brooklyn. The crowns were on images of Jesus Christ and Mary his mother.

I've an idea if Jesus were here his sympathies would be with the thieves and not with the Pharisees who crowned him with gold and jewels.

The only crown he ever wore was one of thorns placed there by emissaries of the Roman emperor and Jewish priesthood. He came to help the lowly and the downtrodden. But since Constantine the Great he has been taken over by the Despots of both Church and State. . . .

—diary, June 1, 1952
(see CHURCH, PRAYER, RELIGION)

JOB

Harry Truman rose to the top by doing a good job—that is how he saw it. He told his daughter: "It's been my policy to do every job assigned to me just a little better than anyone else has done it."

JOHNSON, ANDREW
(U.S. President 1865–1869)

The most underrated president, according to Harry Truman, was Andrew Johnson, Lincoln's successor (with whom Truman probably identified as FDR's successor).

"If Lincoln had lived, he would have done no better than Johnson," Truman said of the seventeenth president. "I guess next to George Washington, the most tolerant and enlightened man in the White House. . . .

"He had plenty of nerve and he knew what he wanted to do and he was willing to make decisions. . . .

"Johnson did his level best to be a constitutional president, and he knew more about the constitution than any man ever in the White House."

KENNEDY, JACQUELINE

I first learned that President Kennedy had been shot while visiting Kansas City at the Muehlebach Hotel. I did not know at that time that he had been killed. This I learned a short time later while I was in the car. . . . As I was preparing to fly to Washington, I received a call from President Johnson telling me that a plane was being sent for me and I was able to arrive the day before the funeral. I went directly to the Blair House.

Shortly after arriving there we rode over to the White House to call on Mrs. Kennedy. I found her as I had expected, remarkably self possessed and poised, but to me the deep sadness in her eyes came through. She said to me her husband, the President, spoke of me often and with much feeling and understanding of what we tried to do, and I found myself choked up with emotion.

It is difficult for one who has lived through the Presidency in the many trials and burdens that go with it, not to realize the enormity of the tragedy that had befallen the nation and the tragic blow that was visited on his family, and particularly on the wife of the President.

—desk note, October 5, 1964

KENNEDY, JOHN F.
(U.S. President 1961–1963)

Harry Truman charged that Joe Kennedy "bought" the Democratic nomination for his son.

"It's not the Pope I'm afraid of," Truman remarked, "it's the Pop."

After the 1960 Democratic convention, Truman wrote to Dean Acheson:

"At the convention, Jack Kennedy won the nomination. I'm from Missouri, you know, and I have to be shown. Well, Kennedy showed me."

Before long Harry Truman was saying: "I think that young fella might just make a hell of a fine president."

Truman campaigned for John F. Kennedy in 1960, but caused an uproar when it was reported in the Associated Press that he said, "Anyone who voted for Nixon and Lodge ought to go to hell."

After Nixon made Truman's profanity an issue, JFK wrote to Truman: "Dear Mr. President, I have noted your suggestion as to where those who vote for my opponent shall go. While I understand and sympathize with your deep motivation, I think it's important that our side refrain from raising the religious question."

Two years later Truman wrote a letter to President Kennedy:

June 28, 1962

Dear Mr. President:

It looks as if the Republicans haven't changed a bit since 1936. Pres. Roosevelt had his troubles with them—so did I.

Mr. President, you are on the right track. Don't let them tell *you* what to do—you tell them, as you have.

Your suggestions for the public welfare, in my opinion, are correct.

You know my program was "Give 'em Hell" and if they don't like it give 'em more hell.

Sincerely, Harry S. Truman

KISS

Harry Truman was a good student, but not the best in his graduating high school. Valedictorian honors went to his friend Charlie Ross. After the graduation ceremony, their English teacher, Matilda "Tillie" Brown, bestowed a kiss upon Ross.

When classmates expressed jealousy over this kiss, Miss Brown justified it. "Whoever earned a kiss would get one," she said. Ross received the only kiss that day from Tillie Brown.

Forty-odd years later, President Truman hired Charlie Ross as his presidential press secretary.

"Say," Charlie said, "won't this be news for Miss Tillie?"

President Truman called up Tillie Brown at once. "Miss Brown," he greeted her, "this is the president of the United States. How about that kiss I never got? Have I done something worthwhile enough to rate it now?"

Miss Tillie replied, "You certainly have."

KOREA

Asked what his most difficult decision as President had been, Truman told Edward R. Murrow (in the interview of February 2, 1958) that it was the ordering of the intervention in Korea.

"When the Republic of Korea was about to be overcome by aggressions started by the Communists, backed by

Russia and what later became Communist China, it seemed to me that the proper thing was to establish the United Nations as a going concern and that's what I tried to do."

"Any regrets?" asked Murrow.

"Not the slightest," said Truman, "not the slightest in the world."

L

LEADER

"My definition of a leader in a free country," Truman liked to say, "is a man who can persuade other people to do what they don't want to do and like it."

A successful leader cannot afford to lose the common touch.
—*Quarterly Journal of Speech*, February 1954

LEADERSHIP

I wonder how far Moses would have gone if he'd taken a poll in Egypt? What would Jesus Christ have preached if he'd taken a poll in Israel? Where would the Reformation have gone if Martin Luther had taken a poll? It isn't polls or public opinion of the moment that counts. It is right and wrong and leadership ... that makes epochs in the history of the world.

—memorandum, 1954
(see POLLS)

LEOPARD

Truman was not above name-calling in a hard-fought political campaign. Among other names, nicknames, and slangy sobriquets, he called his opponent Thomas Dewey "the Leopard."

The leopard has not changed his spots—he has merely hired some public relations experts. And they have taught him to wear sheep's clothing and to purr sweet nothings about unity in a soothing voice. But it's the same old leopard.

> —campaign speech, Buffalo, October 8, 1948
> (see DEWEY, THOMAS; DOCTOR DEWEY; DOUBLE-TALK)

LEWIS, JOHN L.

"I wouldn't appoint Lewis to be dog catcher," snapped the President in response to a senator's suggestion that he appoint labor leader John L. Lewis ambassador to the Soviet Union. "He cannot face the music when the tune is not to his liking."

President Truman clashed with John L. Lewis over a miners' strike in 1946. When Lewis defied a court order and called a strike, the President appealed directly to the miners to go back to work. Lewis capitulated and called off the strike.

"Well, John L. had to fold up. He couldn't take the gaff," Truman wrote his mother (using a slang expression that means "to stand the ordeal"). "No bully can."

> (see DEMAGOGUE-CALLING)

LIBERTY

"It was the spirit of liberty which gave us our armed strength and which made our men invincible in battle," declared President Truman proudly on September 1, 1945, after the Japanese surrender. "We now know, that the spirit of liberty, the freedom of the individual, and the personal dignity of man are the strongest and toughest and most enduring forces in the world.

"Liberty does not make all men perfect nor all society secure. But it has provided more solid progress and happiness and decency for more people than any other philosophy of government in history. And this day has shown again that it provides the greatest strength and the greatest power which man has ever reached."

LINCOLN, ABRAHAM
(U.S. President 1861–1865)

"Lincoln was just himself, and that's the sort of man I admire," Truman said of the sixteenth president, his favorite Republican.

"Lincoln *had* to make decisions and take chances, and he studied each situation and made decisions that he felt were best for the people of the United States and for the rest of the world, and that's the reason he turned out to be a great president."

LINCOLN'S GHOST

Before moving into the executive mansion, President Truman asked the White House chief usher, J. B. West, for a guided tour.

When the usher showed him Lincoln's room, stacked with heavy Victorian furniture and a huge bed, Truman asked, "Do we dare evict Mr. Lincoln so my daughter can use it?"

The usher tried to assure him that Mr. Lincoln probably slept in every room of the White House. He recounted how many times Truman's predecessors had moved furniture from one room to another, including the Lincoln room.

"Now I know why they say Lincoln's ghost walks around up here at night," Truman remarked. "He's looking for his bed."

(see GHOSTS)

LOYALTY OATHS

"I think a test oath for students is silly," Truman replied when asked about a proposed requirement that all students receiving government assistance take a loyalty oath. "Teachers who don't know enough to teach you about our great government have no business being teachers, and after you've learned all you can about it, if you become one who doesn't appreciate his government, you are welcome to go to Russia or somewhere else, and then you can satisfy yourself."

LUCE, CLARE BOOTHE

Clare Boothe Luce, a Republican congresswoman from Connecticut, made some critical, caustic remarks about Bess Truman during the 1944 campaign (dubbing her "Payroll Bess"), arousing the ire of Harry Truman.

"The way she talked about my wife," Truman told a reporter, "well, if she were a man, I would have done something about it."

When he became president Truman refused to invite Mrs. Luce to any White House functions.

In 1948 Clare Boothe Luce confidently predicted that Truman would lose to Dewey, saying: "He is a gone goose." Of course, Truman did not lose. He joked privately that the glamorous Mrs. Luce spelled her name L-O-O-S-E.

LUCE, HENRY

Henry Luce, founding editor of *Time*, went to the White House in 1945 to ask why his wife, Clare Boothe Luce, was barred from the executive mansion. Truman, as reported by Harry Vaughn, gave this answer:

"Mr. Luce, you've asked a fair question and I'll give you a fair answer. I've been in politics thirty-five years and everything that could be said about a human being has been said about me. But my wife has never been in politics. She has always conducted herself in a circumspect manner and no one has a right to make derogatory remarks about her. Now your wife has said many unkind and untrue things about Mrs. Truman. And as long as I'm in residence here, she'll not be a guest at the White House."

(see also TRUMAN, BESS)

M

MACARTHUR, DOUGLAS

President Truman met with General MacArthur on Wake Island on October 12, 1950, to discuss the inflammatory Korean situation. At the beginning of their first meeting, the general asked if the President "minded" if he smoked his pipe.

"No," Truman answered. "I suppose I have had more smoke blown at me than any other man alive."

Truman's decision to fire MacArthur for insubordination proved to be his most controversial act as Commander-in-Chief.

When a reporter remarked that it took guts to fire MacArthur, the President shrugged it off. "Courage didn't have anything to do with it. General MacArthur was insubordinate and I fired him. That's all there was to it."

Privately, Truman referred to "Mac" as "our great bald-headed general, with the dyed hair" and described him (in a private memorandum dated June 17, 1945) as "Mr. Prima Donna, Brass Hat, Five Star MacArthur. He's worse than the Cabots and the Lodges—at least they talked with one another before they told God what to do. Mac tells God right off."

Among the White House staff was circulated a mock "Schedule for Welcoming General MacArthur to Washington."

12:30	Wades ashore from Snorkel submarine
12:40	Parade to the Capitol with General MacArthur riding an elephant
1:00	General MacArthur addresses Members of Congress
1:30–1:49	Applause for General MacArthur
1:50	Burning of the Constitution
2:00	21-atomic bomb salute
3:00	Basket Lunch, Monument Grounds

MADISON, JAMES
(U.S. President 1809–1817)

The thirty-third president's evaluation of the fourth president, James Madison:

"When he became president, he was like every other man of considerable brain power and education: He found it difficult to make decisions."

MARINES

The Marine Corps is the Navy's police force and as long as I am President that is what it will remain. They have a propaganda machine that is almost equal to Stalin's.

—quoted in *Time*, September 18, 1950
(Truman later apologized for the remark)

MARSHALL, GENERAL GEORGE

The more I see . . . the more certain I am he's the great one of the age.

—note on appointment sheet, February 18, 1947

MARSHALL PLAN

In 1947 President Truman and his top aides developed a massive plan for rebuilding western Europe. Winston Churchill called it "the most unsordid act in history." Officially it was called the European Recovery Program, a title that never caught on with the press.

Clark Clifford suggested it be called the Truman Plan.

Truman vetoed the idea. "Are you crazy?" he said. "If we sent it up to that Republican Congress with my name on it, they'd tear it apart. We're going to call it the Marshall Plan."

The program was announced by Secretary of State George Marshall in a commencement speech at Harvard.

"He was right," Clifford concluded years later. "But I still think it deserved to be called the Truman Plan."

MARSHALS

President Truman brought an old Missouri friend, Fred Canfil, to the Potsdam Conference in July 1945. One day after a meeting, Truman called Canfil over and introduced him to Stalin.

"Marshal Stalin, I want you to meet Marshal Canfil," Truman introduced them, without explaining that he had recently appointed Canfil a federal marshal in Missouri.

After that introduction, Marshal Canfil was treated with great respect by all the members of the Russian delegation.

MATERIAL THINGS

Material things are ashes, if there is no spiritual background for the support of those material things.

—public papers, 1950

McCARTHY, JOSEPH

On February 9, 1950, Senator Joseph McCarthy made the historic announcement that he had obtained a list of names of Communists in the Department of State. This signaled the beginning of an era of accusation and suspicion—the McCarthy era.

"There were no Communists in the State Department," Truman scoffed. "That was a bunch of hooey and it never was proved. McCarthy started out with 105, and then got down to 80, then down to 30, then down to 12, and then didn't find any."

During a meeting with advisors, President Truman asked for ideas on how to fight the spread of McCarthyism. One aide mentioned that a dossier had been compiled of evidence of the Wisconsin Senator's illicit affairs with women. Releasing this information would ruin McCarthy's career.

Truman would not allow it. He explained it this way:

"Nobody, not even the president of the United States, can approach too close to a skunk, in skunk territory, and expect to get anything out of it except a bad smell."

I think the greatest asset that the Kremlin has is Senator McCarthy.

—to a reporter, March 30, 1950

McCARTHYISM

McCarthyism . . . the meaning of the word is the corruption of truth, the abandonment of our historical devotion to fair play. It is the abandonment of "due process" of law. It is the use of the big lie and the unfounded accusation against any citizen in the name of Americanism and security.

It is the rise to power of the demagogue who lives on untruth; it is the spread of fear and the destruction of faith in every level of our society.

My friends, this is not a partisan matter. This horrible cancer is eating at the vitals of America and it can destroy the great edifice of freedom.

—televised address, Kansas City, November 17, 1953

McKINLEYISM

Harry Truman considered President Eisenhower politically backward. Asked about Ike's economic policy, Truman had two words for it:

"Creeping McKinleyism!"

(see EISENHOWER, DWIGHT)

MEAT AND POTATOES

"I'm a meat and potatoes man."

This was a favorite expression of Harry Truman, who preferred to dine and define himself simply.

MEMORIALS

I am not in favor of erecting memorials to people who are living. I think it's bad business because a person may do something before he dies that will make the people want to tear the memorial down.

—memorandum, 1948

MEXICO

During a trip to Mexico to discuss the Good Neighbor Policy, President Truman made a gesture that brought tears to the eyes of many Mexicans. Margaret Truman recalled it in her biography:

> My father drew upon his knowledge of history for a gesture that aroused the deepest emotions in the Mexican people. He suddenly announced he wanted to visit Chapultepec. The State Department types in the American embassy were aghast. Almost exactly one hundred years ago, the American army had stormed this fortress in its successful assault on Mexico City. Among the Mexican garrison had been several hundred young cadets who fought to the last man, with incredible bravery. A handful of them—six, I believe—were trapped on the roof and committed suicide by leaping over the walls rather than surrender. A shrine to *Los Niños Heroes* had been erected by the Mexican people in Chapultepec.
>
> After touring the fortress my father went straight to this shrine and placed a wreath before it. Then he stood with bowed head, paying silent tribute to the memory of these young men who had died so heroically for their country. A contingent of contemporary cadets was drawn up in precise military formation, and when they saw the President of the United States make this almost unbelievable (to them) gesture, tears streamed down their cheeks. "Brave men do not belong to any one country," Dad said. "I respect bravery wherever I see it."

MILITARY LEADERS

"The only military hero who really made a good president was George Washington, and he was not really a professional soldier," Truman wrote in reflection on military leaders as national leaders.

"I think history has proven that professional military

men have trouble running a free government. Because the professional military man is used most of the time to being a dictator."

One reason that we have been so careful to keep the military within its own preserve is that the very nature of the service hierarchy gives military commanders little if any opportunity to learn the humility that is needed for good public service.

—*Memoirs, Vol. 2*, 1956
(see GENERALS; GRANT, ULYSSES; EISENHOWER, DWIGHT)

MILITARY WASTE

"They do a good job on the waste side," Truman observed as chairman of the Special Committee to Investigate the National Defense Program. "They throw money around by the scoop shovelful."

MINIMUM WAGE

The Republicans favor a minimum wage—the smaller the minimum the better.

—Akron, October 11, 1948
(see REPUBLICANS)

MISSOURI

"Now Missouri has had a number of notorious characters," mused the retired president in a lecture at Columbia University on April 27, 1959. "The three, I guess, most notorious are Mark Twain, Jesse James, and me. Mark and Jesse are dead and I have to fill in for them, so here I am."

(see RAILROAD ROBBERY; TWAIN, MARK)

MISSOURI WALTZ

Most people assumed that Missouri's most famous citizen was fond of "The Missouri Waltz." But it was not so. "It's a ragtime song and if you let me say what I think, I don't give a damn about it," Truman confessed to Edward R. Murrow in 1958, "but I can't say it out loud because it's the song of Missouri. It's as bad as 'The Star Spangled Banner' as far as music is concerned."

(see NIXON, RICHARD)

MISTAKES

I am sometimes accused of claiming credit for every good thing that happened in the United States while I have been President, and, by the same token, accused of never admitting a mistake. As for the mistakes, I know that I make them like everybody else does, and I do admit them from time to time. However, it has not seemed necessary for me to spend a great deal of time calling attention to my mistakes because there have always been plenty of people who were willing to do that for me.

—remarks, Philadelphia, September 16, 1952

But when I make a mistake it is a good one.

—letter to mother and sister, September 18, 1944

MOLOTOV, VYACHESLAV

The new American President spoke rather roughly with Soviet foreign minister Vyacheslav Molotov during their talks on April 23 and April 24, 1945. Truman took the Russians to task for their violations of the Yalta agreement and demanded that they keep their word.

"We don't want to operate on the basis of a one-way street," stated President Truman sternly.

"I have never been talked to like that in my life," replied a flushed, ruffled Molotov, unaccustomed to such directness.

The President snapped, "Carry out your agreements and you won't get talked to like that."

Truman later described Molotov as "a perfect mutton head."

MONEY

One of the difficulties, as I see it, is that we worship money instead of honor. A billionaire in our estimation is much greater in the eyes of the people than the public servant who works for the public interest. It makes no difference if the billionaire rode to wealth on the sweat of little children and the blood of underpaid labor. . . .

No one ever considered Carnegie libraries steeped in the blood of the Homestead steel workers, but they are. We do not remember that the Rockefeller Foundation is founded on the dead miners of the Colorado Fuel & Iron Company and a dozen other similar performances.

We worship mammon; and until we go back to ancient fundamentals and return to the Giver of the Tables of the Law and His teachings, these conditions are going to remain with us.

—speech to Congress, December 20, 1937

MONEY MAKING

"There was never one of our name who had sense enough to make money," admitted Harry Truman, who lost money on more than one ill-fated business enterprise in his younger years. "I am no exception."

(see BIOGRAPHY 1919–1922)

MORNING

"Most people don't know when the best part of the day is," Truman told reporters. "It's the early morning."

(see EARLY, WALKING)

MOTHER

When her son Harry was nominated for the Vice-Presidency in 1944, a cousin, General Ralph Truman, remarked to Mrs. Truman how proud she must be of her son. Martha Truman simply smiled and said, "Oh, well, I liked him just as well before."

Harry Truman inherited some of his crusty wit from his mother, of whom he recalled fondly:

"One of the funniest things she said when I brought her to Washington in the plane and got her off at the airport and all the photographers and newsmen crowded around her was, 'Oh, fiddlesticks, why didn't you tell me about this, and I would have stayed home.' "

MULE

"My favorite animal is the mule," wrote Truman in *Mr. Citizen* (1960) after retiring from active politics. "He has more sense than a horse. He knows when to stop eating— and when to stop working."

MUSIC

"I don't like noise that passes for music today," Truman told William Hillman in an interview. "Maybe I'm old-fashioned. I like something with a tune or melody to it.

"Did you ever sit and listen to an orchestra play a fine overture and imagine that things were as they ought to be and not as they are? Music that I can understand always makes me feel that way."

MUSIC CRITIC

About the only time I ever acted when I was really out of sorts was when I told a music critic where to get off when he said some mean things about my daughter. If I had thought about it, I probably wouldn't have done it.

—interview with Edward R. Murrow, February 2, 1958
(see HUME, PAUL)

NATION

When a nation ceases to have something to struggle for it usually gets fat and dies of a heart ailment just like a human being does.

—memorandum, 1951

NATIONAL HEALTH

When we find that 34% of our young men and women are unfit for military service because of physical and mental defects, there is something wrong with the health of the country and I am trying to find a remedy for it.

—letter to Dr. Sam E. Roberts, September 8, 1949

NATIONAL HEALTH CARE

President Truman's national health care proposals met with strong opposition—especially from the healthy and the wealthy, he noted:

"I usually find that those who are loudest in protesting against medical help by the federal government are those who do not need help."

We are rightly proud of the high standards of medical care we know how to provide in the United States. The fact is, however, that most of our people cannot afford to pay for the care they need. I have often and strongly urged that this condition demands a national health program. The heart of the program must be a national system of payment for medical care based on well-tried insurance principles. This great nation cannot afford to allow its citizens to suffer needlessly from the lack of proper medical care.

—message to Congress, January 7, 1948
(see HEALTH INSURANCE, BIOGRAPHY 1966)

NATIVE AMERICANS

"How would I mark our paper in terms of the Indian? Zero minus," Truman said sadly. "If you want to talk about one hundred percent Americans, you must go back to the inhabitants of the United States at the time that Europeans first landed. . . ."

"The treatment of the Indians by the white settlers of both South America and North America was a disgrace and always will be. . . . The list of mistreatment and treachery toward the Indians is almost endless. Practically every great chief ended up murdered or a prisoner.

"The Indians didn't understand the approach of the white man in business dealings, and they got cheated every time they got into a trade with the white man."

Some of the greatest leaders this country ever produced were the leaders of the Indian tribes.

—*Where the Buck Stops* (Margaret Truman, ed.), 1989
(see OOMPAH)

NECKTIE

A television crew asked to reshoot part of an interview with the former President about his decision to intervene in Korea.

The producer pointed out that Truman was wearing a different necktie now from the one he had on originally.

"Does it *really* matter?" Truman asked. "Because if while I'm talking about Korea people are asking each other about my necktie, it seems to me we're in a great deal of trouble."

NEW DEAL

Republican speakers have talked a great deal about the cost of the New Deal. I have never heard one of them speak derogatorily of the cost of the World War. . . . I do not understand a mind which sees a gracious benefice in spending money to slay and maim human beings in almost unimaginable amounts and deprecates the expenditure of a smaller sum to patch up the ills of erring mankind.

—Senate campaign speech, October 12, 1934

NEWS

Lies and mud make "news"—the truth and flowers do not.
—letter to his cousin Ethel Noland, September 24, 1950

News should never be edited. Editorials should be frankly the opinions of the owners and publishers, and should be so stated. But news should be reported as it happened.
—desk note, written in the 1950s, found after death

NEWSPAPER PUBLISHERS

A reporter once reminded Truman of an admired presidential predecessor's generosity toward the press: "Mr. President, the first thing Jefferson did was to release eleven newspaper publishers from prison."

"Yes," President Truman nodded. "I think he made a mistake on that."

(see COLUMNISTS; JEFFERSON, THOMAS; PUBLISHERS)

NEWSPAPERS

"Most people don't think for themselves," Truman commented, "they lean on newspapers."

NIXON, RICHARD
(U.S. President 1969–1974)

Truman reserved some of his bluntest language for his Republican adversary Richard Nixon, whom he regarded as a spokesman for special interests.

"I don't like Nixon and I never will," he admitted frankly. "Mr. Nixon lacks the moral sensitivity which the occupant of the White House should possess ... he is impetuous, quick to act, rash, and on occasions his conduct is irresponsible."

When Nixon was elected Vice-President, Truman warned: "He is a dangerous man. Never has there been one like him so close to the presidency."

During the 1960 campaign Truman was reported by the Associated Press as having said that "anyone who voted for Nixon and Lodge ought to go to hell" and that Nixon "doesn't know the difference between telling the truth and lying." Later Truman denied making the first statement, but added, "They can't challenge the second."

Soon after Nixon's election as thirty-seventh President,

he paid a visit to the thirty-third president in Independence, Missouri. Truman, now eighty-four and in ill health, met Nixon at the Truman Library. Nixon immediately sat down at the piano and played "The Missouri Waltz" in tribute, not knowing how much Truman disliked the song. Truman, hard of hearing, showed no reaction until Nixon finished, then turned to Bess and asked: "What was it?"

(see MISSOURI WALTZ)

NOTORIETY

Men often mistake notoriety for fame, and would rather be remarked for their vices and follies than not to be noticed at all!

—from his letters and memoranda of 1950

NUTS

"There are immense numbers of nuts in the USA," declared President Truman after his mother shipped him a batch of "screwball letters."

O

OLD-FASHIONEDS

The Trumans liked to have a cocktail before dinner, and Mrs. Truman was very particular about how their old-fashioneds should be prepared.

"Can you make the old-fashioneds a little drier?" she asked the White House butler, Alonzo Fields.

Fields, who considered himself a good bartender, tried another recipe. The Trumans said nothing to Fields, but the next morning Mrs. Truman told J. B. West, the chief usher, "They make the worst old-fashioneds here I've ever tasted. They're like fruit punch."

Fields got the word from West. That evening when Mrs. Truman rang for him, the butler dumped two big splashes of bourbon over ice and served it up to the Trumans, without fruit slices or bitters.

Mrs. Truman tasted the drink and smiled: "Now that's the way we like our old-fashioneds."

(see TRUMAN, BESS)

OOMPAH

Truman liked to tell the story of how the Native Americans shouted "Oompah!" during his campaign speech on an Indian reservation in New Mexico.

As he told the Native Americans why they should vote for him, they gestured and shouted "Oompah!" excitedly.

After the speech, Truman was led across a corral that had been filled with horses.

"Careful," his Indian guide warned him, "don't step in the oompah!"

(see HORSE MANURE)

OPERATION

"They are still trying to hold me down," Truman reported to a friend after a minor operation. "The doctor still has his foot on my neck and he's getting a lot of help from Mrs. Truman and Margaret."

(see COLD)

OPPOSITION

You don't have to worry about where I stand. You know! I want you to see whether you can find out where the opposition stands. I'll bet you can't.

—speech, Fresno, California, September 23, 1948

ORATORS

The greatest orators . . . understood what they wanted to say, said it in short sentences and said it quickly and then got out of there before people fell asleep.

—*Where the Buck Stops* (Margaret Truman, ed.), 1989

P

PAY-AS-YOU-GO

Pay-as-you-go in practice is not as popular as borrow-and-owe, but Truman swore by it. "There is nothing sacred about the pay-as-you-go idea so far as I am concerned," he explained, "except that it represents the soundest principle of financing that I know."

PEACE

"The simple truth is hard to learn," Truman told biographer William Hillman, "and that is, it is in the interest of people to keep the peace."

Peace is more complicated than war, Truman explained. It requires the cooperation of more than one nation. "It takes only one nation to make war," he said. "But it takes two or more to make a peace. . . .

"A just and lasting peace cannot be attained by diplomatic agreement alone, or by military cooperation alone.

Experience has shown how deeply the seeds of war are planted by economic rivalry and by social injustice. . . .

"We can well afford to pay the price of peace. Our only alternative is to pay the terrible cost of war."

Truman wrote in his *Memoirs* (1956): "There is enough in the world for everyone to have plenty to live on happily and to be at peace with his neighbors. . . . I believe, as I said on January 15, 1953, in my last address to the American people before leaving the White House: 'We have averted World War III up to now, and we may have already succeeded in establishing conditions which can keep that war from happening as far ahead as man can see.' "

Peace is the goal of my life. I'd rather have lasting peace in the world than be President. I wish for peace, I work for peace and I pray for peace continually.

—Philadelphia, October 6, 1948

We knew that there could be no lasting peace so long as there were large populations in the world living under primitive conditions and suffering from starvation, disease, and denial of the advantages of modern science and industry.

—Preface, *Memoirs, Vol. 2*, 1956

I don't believe that because peace is difficult that war is inevitable.

—public papers, 1948

We must face the fact that peace must be built upon power, as well as upon good will and good deeds.

—public papers, 1945

The desire for peace is futile unless there is enough strength ready and willing to enforce that desire in any emergency.

—public papers, 1945

Sherman was wrong. I'm telling you I find peace is hell.

—humorous speech at Gridiron Dinner, December 1946 (referring to the decline in Truman's popularity since the war ended)

PENDERGAST, T. J.

"I was about as popular as a skunk in the parlor," Truman recalled of his days of association with the political machine of Missouri "boss" T. J. Pendergast, with whom Truman was often accused of conspiring.

"He's the contrariest man on earth," T. J. Pendergast said of Truman, with whom he often clashed.

Accused of being cronies with Pendergast, Truman refused to apologize for their friendship and defended Pendergast to the end.

"We don't play halfway politics in Missouri," Truman explained in a memorandum written in 1949. "When we start out with a man, if he is any good at all, we always stay with him to the end. Sometimes people quit me but I never quit people when I start to back them up."

(see ACHESON, DEAN; FRIEND)

PENS

The Truman sense of humor was illustrated by a visit to Colgate University, where the ex-president presented each of the student leaders with a pen inscribed:

"I swiped this from Harry S. Truman."

PEOPLE

"I like people and I like to be among them," affirmed Harry Truman. "I like to gossip with friends. I like to exchange views and opinions with people in all walks of life."

He added: "If you don't like people, you hadn't ought to be in politics."

PESSIMISTS

"I grew up to look for the good in people," Truman said, looking back. "I have never regarded people with suspicion—for such an attitude usually leads to worrying yourself into being a pessimist about everything, people included. . . .

"I have never seen pessimists make anything work, or contribute anything of lasting value."

PHYSICAL FITNESS

"You can't be mentally fit," Truman told writer John Hersey, "unless you're physically fit."

PIANO PLAYER

Harry Truman loved to play the piano and often surprised guests with a keyboard display.

"My choice early in life was either to be a piano player in a whorehouse or a politician," Truman would sometimes tell male visitors to the White House. Pausing, he would add: "To tell the truth, there's hardly a difference."

On one occasion in Caruthersville, Missouri, he was asked to play Paderewski's "Minuet." Truman sat down at the piano, turned to his audience, and said:

"When Stalin heard me play this, he signed the protocol."

Truman often charmed and disarmed people with his piano playing prowess, but it could get him into trouble. When he was Vice-President he posed for a publicity photo with actress Lauren Bacall. The widely reproduced news photo showed the sultry actress with a seductive look, perched on top of a piano being played by Harry Truman.

When the Vice-President was asked what his wife Bess said when she saw this photo, Truman answered, "She said she thought it was time for me to quit playing the piano."

(see POTSDAM)

111

PICASSO, PABLO

Truman wasted little praise on modern art, or its most prominent practitioner, Pablo Picasso, whom he dismissed as "a French Communist caricaturist."

(see ART GALLERIES)

PICTURES

"They say pictures don't lie, but they do," the ex-president told Merle Miller. "Pictures can lie just as much as words, if that's what the big editors and publishers set out to do."

PIERCE, FRANKLIN
(U.S. President 1853–1857)

"Pierce was a nincompoop."

In a word Truman summed up his opinion of Franklin Pierce, the fourteenth president.

"Franklin Pierce was a good-looking man from New Hampshire who did not have to work for the presidency in 1852. . . . Glamour has often played an active role in the selection of American presidents. Pierce, like Harding, was chosen partly because 'he looked like a president.' . . . Though he looked the way people who make movies think a president should look, he didn't pay any more attention to business as president of the United States than the man in the moon, and he really made a mess of things."

PLAN

Keep working on a plan. Make no little plans. Make the biggest one you can think of, and spend the rest of your life carrying it out. You can always amend a big plan, but you can never expand a little one. I don't believe in little plans.

—public papers, 1949

POETS

"I've always—and I hadn't ought to say this, had a lot more faith in poets than in reporters," Truman informed biographer Merle Miller. "Reporters just tell what has happened, and they don't do too good a job of it a lot of the time, but poets, some of them, they write about what's going to happen."

Harry Truman carried in his wallet a well-worn quotation from a poem by the Victorian English poet Alfred Tennyson, "Locksley Hall." He had been carrying it since his high school graduation in 1901. "The paper I copied it on kept wearing out, and I kept recopying it. I don't know how many times, twenty or thirty I expect."

These were the lines Truman copied over and over again:

For I dipp'd into the future, far as human eye could see,
Saw the Vision of the world, and all the wonder that would be;
Saw the heavens fill with commerce, argosies of magic sails,
Pilots of the purple twilight, dropping down with costly bales;
Heard the heavens filled with shouting,
    and there rain'd a ghastly dew
From the nations' airy navies grappling in the central blue;
Far along the world-wide whisper of the south-wind rushing
    warm,
With the standards of the people plunging through the thunder-storm;
Till the war drum throbb'd no longer and the battle flags were
    furled
In the Parliament of man, the Federation of the world.
There the common sense of most shall hold a fretful realm in
    awe,
And the kindly earth shall slumber, lapp'd in universal law.

"That poem made a very strong impression on me," Truman recalled, "because, although it was written in 1840 or thereabouts, it predicted a great many things that happened during my lifetime and some other things that haven't happened yet but will happen someday."

POLITICIAN

"I'm just a politician from Missouri and proud of it," Harry Truman liked to say in his humble yet confident way.

After announcing he would not run for reelection in 1952, President Truman remarked, "I think there comes a time when every politician, whether he be in a country, state, or federal office, should retire. Most of them find it impossible to do that—they either have to be carried out feet first or kicked out."

Soon after retiring and returning to Independence in 1953, Truman wrote in reflection on the role of the politician:

> It takes a life time of the hardest kind of work and study to become a successful politician. . . .
>
> A great politician is known for the service he renders. . . .
>
> No young man should go into politics if he wants to get rich or if he expects an adequate reward for his services. An honest public servant can't become rich in politics. He can only attain greatness and satisfaction by service.

My definition of a politician is . . . [one] who understands "Government" and who knows how to make it work.

—letter to Arthur Schlesinger Jr., September 1960

I'm proud to be a politician. A politician is a man who understands government, and it takes a politician to run a government.

—*New York World-Telegram & Sun*, April 12, 1958

You can tell a good politician by how sincere he is in liking and wanting to help people.

—*Mr. President*, 1960

A politician soon learns that his performance on the stage depends as much on the stagehands as on his own skill.

—*Memoirs, Vol. 2*, 1956
(see PUBLIC SERVANT, STATESMAN)

POLITICS

"Politics is a fascinating game, because politics is government. It is the art of government," Truman wrote in retirement.

"I never ran for a political office I wanted. But I've fought for every one I've ever had. Damn it! I've never had an office I didn't have to fight for, tooth or nail."

I have always defined politics to mean the science of government, perhaps the most important science because it involves the art and ability of people to live together.

—*Memoirs, Vol. 2*, 1956

Politics—good politics—is public service. There is no life or occupation in which a man can find a greater opportunity to serve his community or his country.

—from President's Secretary's files, Box 333, written in 1953

POLK, JAMES
(U.S. President 1845–1849)

"Polk was a man who knew what he wanted to do and did it," Truman assessed the eleventh President. "He was an executive like we dream about, and very seldom see . . .

"He is one man who has been very much overlooked in the history of our country. He made that statement when he ran that he would not run for a second term. He put his program through in that four year term and retired to die three months and eleven days later."

—*Memoirs, Vol. 2*, 1956

POLLS

Truman, who consistently lagged behind his opponent Dewey in the polls, defied the polls in a campaign speech in Cleveland on October 26, 1948:

"Polls are like sleeping pills designed to lull the voters into sleeping on election day. You might call them sleeping polls. The same doctor I told you about the other night in Pittsburgh—the Republican candidate—keeps handing out these sleeping polls, and some people have been taking them. This doctor keeps telling the people, 'Don't worry, take a poll and go to sleep.' But most of the people are not being fooled. They know that sleeping polls are bad for the system. They affect the mind. An overdose could be fatal."

Truman made his own prediction about the pollsters. "Wait until the morning of November 3 [the day after the 1948 election], and you are going to see more red-faced pollsters than you ever looked at in your life!"

Those words proved to be prophetic. No one was more surprised by Truman's upset victory over Dewey on November 2, 1948, than the pollsters.

(see LEADERSHIP)

POTSDAM

Before leaving for the historic Potsdam Conference, President Truman wrote his mother on July 3, 1945:

"I am getting ready to see Stalin & Churchill, and it is a chore. I have to take my tuxedo, tails ... preacher coat, high hat, low hat, and hard hat."

The meeting of Churchill, Stalin, and Truman occurred in Potsdam, a village in Germany, where they negotiated postwar arrangements in Germany and combined strategy against the still-undefeated Japanese.

"Churchill talks all the time and Stalin just grunts but

you know what he means," Truman wrote home on July 18, 1945.

A few days later he jotted down in a private memorandum: "I was having as much difficulty with Prime Minister Churchill as I was having with Stalin ... it was my opinion that each of them was trying to make me the paw of the cat that pulled the chestnuts out of the fire."

After it was all over, Truman recalled Potsdam in a letter to Dean Acheson: "What a show it was! But a large number of agreements were reached in spite of the setup—only to be broken as soon as the unconscionable Russian Dictator returned to Moscow! And I liked the little son of a bitch. He was a good six inches shorter than I am and even Churchill was only three inches taller than Joe. Yet I was the little man in stature and intellect! Well we'll see."

(see CHURCHILL, WINSTON; STALIN, JOSEPH)

POWER

There is a lure in power. It can get into a man's blood just as gambling and lust for money have been known to do.

—diary, April 16, 1950

PRAYER

Harry Truman's favorite prayer, "a prayer said over & over all my life from eighteen years old and younger," was handwritten in pencil, dated 8/15/50. "The prayer on this page has been said by me—by Harry S. Truman—from high school days, as window washer, bottle duster, floor scrubber in an Independence, Mo., drugstore, as a timekeeper on a railroad contract gang, as an employee of a newspaper, as a bank clerk, as a farmer riding a gang plow behind four horses and mules, as a fraternity official learning to say nothing at all if good could not be said of a man, as a public official judging the weaknesses and short-

117

comings of constituents, and as President of the United States of America."

Oh! Almighty and Everlasting God, Creator of Heaven, Earth and the Universe:

Help me to be, to think, to act what is right, because it is right; make me truthful, honest and honorable in all things; make me intellectually honest for the sake of right and honor and without thought of reward to me. Give me the ability to be charitable, forgiving and patient with my fellow men—help me to understand their motives and their shortcomings—even as thou understandest mine! Amen, Amen, Amen.

PRESIDENCY

"If you ever pray, pray for me now," President Truman exhorted reporters at his first presidential press conference on April 13, 1945, following the sudden death of FDR.

"I don't know whether you fellows ever had a load of hay fall on you, but when they told me yesterday what had happened, I felt like the moon, the stars, and all the planets had fallen on me. I've got the most terribly responsible job a man ever had."

Truman learned quickly—he had to. "Within the first few months, I discovered that being a President is like riding a tiger. A man has to keep on riding or be swallowed."

During his last year in office, Truman expressed his weariness with the job, writing in his diary on February 18, 1952, a cynical description of the president's role: "He is the No. 1 public relations man of the Government. He spends a lot of time persuading people to do what they should do without persuasion."

Perhaps the most irksome thing about the presidency to Truman was all the second-guessing done by critics, columnists, and so-called experts. One night he wrote an ironic memo for private circulation:

"I have appointed a secretary of columnists. His duties are to listen to all radio commentators, read all columnists in the newspapers from ivory tower to lowest gossip, coordinate them and give me the results so I can run the United States and the world as it should be."

After leaving office, Truman looked back with humility but without regret. "There are a great many people—I suppose a million in this country—who could have done the job better than I did it. But I had the job and I had to do it."

When I was President, every Tom, Dick and Harry tried to tell me what to do.

> —letter to Pierce Adams (who wrote urging the President to complain to the owner of the Kansas City baseball team on their lack of winning), August 14, 1963

The President represents the government to the people, yet is an "outsider" to government insiders. You see, the Generals and the Admirals and the career men in government look upon the occupant of the White House as only a temporary nuisance who soon will be succeeded by another temporary occupant who won't find out what it is all about for a long time, and then it will be too late to do anything about it.

> —letter to Arthur Krock, October 7, 1951 (unsent)

Our government cannot function properly unless the President is master in his own house . . .

> —remarks, New York City, May 8, 1954

A president needs political understanding to *run* the government, but he may be *elected* without it.

> —*Memoirs, Vol. 2*, 1956

You have to know something to be a president. You have got to be a jack-of-all-trades and know something about all of them.

—*Truman Speaks*, 1960

A president cannot always be popular. He has to be able to say *yes* and more often *no*.

—*Memoirs, Vol. 2*, 1956

If a president isn't in an occasional fight with the Congress or the courts, he's not doing a good job.

—*Where the Buck Stops*, 1989

A president may dismiss the abuse of scoundrels, but to be denounced by honest men honestly outraged is a test of greatness that none but the strongest men survive.

—public papers, 1948

Any man who sincerely tries to live up to the responsibilities of the office cannot keep from growing in the presidency.

—*Memoirs, Vol. 2*, 1956

The greatest part of the president's job is to make decisions—big ones and small ones, dozens of them almost every day.

—public papers, 1952–53

To be president of the United States is to be lonely, very lonely at times of great decisions.

—*Memoirs, Vol. 1*, 1955

Lincoln had fits of melancholy. . . . Melancholy goes with the job.

—*The Quotable Truman*, 1994

No president ever had any real rest. Why should I try?

—diary entry, June 30, 1951

PRESIDENTS

"Some of the Presidents were great and some of them weren't," stated Harry Truman matter-of-factly in a lecture at Columbia University on April 27, 1959. "I can say that, because I wasn't one of the great Presidents, but I had a good time trying to be one, I can tell you that."

"I don't think anybody remembers the names of men who attacked Washington on account of the Jay Treaty," Truman wrote in a letter to Max Lowenthal, "nor do they remember the attackers who vilified Jefferson for making the Louisiana Purchase. They almost brought impeachments against him. The same thing is true of Jackson and his efforts to maintain the Union. There never was a man as completely vilified as Lincoln when he took the reins in his own hands."

Presidents have to make decisions if they're going to get anywhere, and those presidents who couldn't make decisions are the ones who caused all the trouble.... The United States has never suffered seriously from any acts of the presidents that were intended for the welfare of the country. It's suffered from the inaction of a great many presidents when actions should have been taken at the right time.

—*Where the Buck Stops,* 1989
(see DECISIONMAKING, WOMEN PRESIDENTS)

PRESIDENTS' RATINGS

A poll of seventy-five historians rated presidents in the July 29, 1962, *New York Times Magazine.* Lincoln, Washington, Franklin D. Roosevelt, Wilson, and Jefferson were rated the greatest in that order, followed by these "near-greats": Jackson, Theodore Roosevelt, Polk, Truman, John Adams, and Cleveland.

Harry Truman was characteristically modest in his response to these ratings. "I don't know how they came to put me so high up on the list but I appreciate it nevertheless. If I had been arranging the first five in the row of the great, I would have put Washington first, Jefferson second, Woodrow Wilson third, Lincoln fourth, and Franklin Roosevelt fifth. I, in all probability, would have moved Andrew Jackson into that row and made six of them. . . ."

(see JACKSON, ANDREW; JEFFERSON, THOMAS; LINCOLN, ABRAHAM; ROOSEVELT, FRANKLIN D.; THEODORE; WASHINGTON, GEORGE)

PRESS

In the fall of 1948 Truman's Republican opponent, Thomas Dewey, was heavily favored. *Fortune* declared: "The prospects of Republican victory are now so overwhelming that an era of what will amount to one party may well impend."

Dewey was leading in the polls. In October *Newsweek* polled fifty political writers to predict the outcome of the election.

On October 12 Clark Clifford stepped off the Truman "whistle-stop" tour train and purchased the *Newsweek* issue with the results of the experts' poll. Huge type proclaimed: FIFTY POLITICAL EXPERTS UNANIMOUSLY PREDICT A DEWEY VICTORY. His heart sank. Clifford tucked the magazine under his coat and returned to the train.

As Clifford walked through the President's car, Truman spotted him and called him over.

"What does it say?"

"What does what say?"

"What have you got under your coat, Clark?"

"Nothing, Mr. President."

"Clark, I saw you get off the train just now and I think that you went in there to see if they had a newsstand with a copy of *Newsweek*. And I think maybe you have it under your coat."

Clifford sighed and handed over the magazine. Truman skimmed the article quickly and handed it back to Clifford calmly.

"Don't worry about that poll, Clark. I know every one of those fifty fellows, and not one of them has enough sense to pound sand into a rathole."

When Truman won the election in defiance of the pundits' predictions, a group of reporters offered to eat crow publicly at a crow-eating dinner in honor of Truman, but the President declined politely.

"Some editors ate crow and left the feathers on," he said later.

Truman could forgive but not forget. "I'm saving up four or five good, hard punches on the nose," he told writer John Hersey, "and when I'm out of this job, I'm going around and delivering them personally."

Truman did not actually carry out that threat, but years after retiring from the White House he was still smarting from press-inflicted wounds. He wrote in his *Memoirs*: "Our means of communicating and consolidating public opinion—the press and the radio—emphasize the differences of opinion rather than agreements. . . .

"If you will study the history of our country you'll find that our greatest presidents and congressional leaders have been the ones who have been vilified worst by the current press. . . .

"When you read what the press had to say about Washington, Jefferson, and Lincoln, and the other presidents, you would think that we never had a decent man in the office since the country began. . . .

"Whenever the press quits abusing me, I know I'm in the wrong pew."

Truman's vigilant regard for the press is illustrated by one occasion when the President was informed that a *Chicago Tribune* writer named Holmes was in Kansas City asking a lot of questions about him and his family. Truman responded, "You might tell the gentleman named Holmes that if he comes out with a pack of lies about Mrs. Truman or any of my family his hide won't hold shucks when I get through with him."

I won both senatorial elections with all the press against me and a presidential election with ninety percent of them against me, all the pollsters, all the "ivory tower" columnists, the gamblers and everybody but the people against me.

> —letter to columnist Bill Southern, July 8, 1949 (unsent)

People in general have lost faith in the modern press and its policies. That is a good thing, too. No one segment should be able to control public opinion.

> —letter to Mr. Roper, pollster, December 30, 1948 (unsent)

The prostitutes of the mind, in my opinion—and it is only one man's—are much more dangerous to the future welfare of mankind than the prostitutes of the body.

> —reply to editorial writer Frank Kent, September 2, 1951

If you have a free press, there's no way in the world for anyone to get by with the subversion of the government.

> —*Where the Buck Stops*, 1989
> (see COLUMNISTS, NEWSPAPER PUBLISHERS)

PRESS CONFERENCE

"A press conference is a kind of show," explained the President to a foreign visitor, "and one of the best there is in Washington."

PRIMA DONNAS

Truman was dismayed at the number of self-important people, or "prima donnas," as he called them, attracted to the seat of power. "I have almost as many prima donnas around me as Roosevelt had," he wrote in a letter to his mother in 1945, "but they are still new at it. They don't get humored as much by me as they did by him. I fire one occasionally and it has a salutary effect."

After a meeting in the East Room with the Roosevelt National Memorial Committee, Truman wrote in his appointment book: "Same bunch of Prima Donnas who helped drive the Boss to his grave are still riding his ghost."

(see ROOSEVELT, FRANKLIN D.)

PRIZE PIG

Attending a junior livestock show in Spokane, Washington, on May 11, 1950, President Truman was almost embarrassed to receive a huge blue ribbon labeled GRAND CHAMPION. He said, slightly chagrined:

"I don't know whether I'm the prize pig or what."

PROBLEM-SOLVING

"It has been my experience in public life that there are few problems which cannot be worked out," Harry Truman concluded after one of the most extraordinarily successful political careers in American history, "if we make a real effort to understand the other fellow's point of view, and if we try to find a solution on the basis of give-and-take, of fairness to both sides."

(see DECISIONMAKING)

PROFITS

In the past profits of the machine have been going to the machine owner. It seems to me that now the profits must be divided more equally with labor.

—speech, Kansas City, Missouri, February 10, 1934
(see NEW DEAL)

PROSPERITY

"We must never forget that prosperity for other people means prosperity for us," Truman told his biographer William Hillman, repeating one of his economic Truman-isms, "and prosperity for us means prosperity for other people."

PUBLIC SCHOOLS

In 1962, when it was a hot political issue, the former president was asked his opinion on federal aid to parochial schools. "If it wasn't for the public schools," Truman replied, "a lot of us would not have an education."

PUBLIC SERVANT

I would much rather be an honorable public servant and known as such than to be the richest man in the world.

—memorandum, July 1954

PUBLIC SPEAKING

"I never use forty dollar words," said Harry Truman, who believed plain talking was the secret of successful public speaking.

"I always made it my business to speak plainly and

directly to the people without indulging in high-powered oratory."

(see ORATORS)

PUBLICITY HOUND

"If a politician is on your side and he gets headlines, that is favorable advertising," Truman once translated the parlance of politics for a layman. "If he is on the other side and gets headlines that are not in your corner, he is a publicity hound."

PUBLISHERS

"I have been told that when a fellow fails at everything else, he either starts a hotel or a newspaper," President Truman teased the audience at a newspaper publishers' association convention.

"In many cases, the publisher only wants talent to present his distorted viewpoint," Truman wrote in a note found in his desk after his death. "Hearst, Pulitzer, Scripps-Howard, Gannett, Bertie McCormick and the Patterson chain are shining examples."

(see COLUMNISTS, NEWSPAPER PUBLISHERS)

PUERTO RICAN INDEPENDENCE

After an assassination attempt on November 1, 1950, by Puerto Rican nationals who desired independence, President Truman did not condemn the Puerto Rican independence movement. Calmly he reiterated a statement he had made in San Juan in 1948:

"The Puerto Rican people should have the right to determine for themselves Puerto Rico's political relationship to the continental United States."

QUESTIONS

Arriving for a vacation in Key West on March 6, 1949, the President's plane touched down before the press plane, which was delayed. President Truman decided to reverse roles with the press for a change. When the press plane landed, Truman met the photographers and reporters at the ramp, welcomed them to Key West, and hastily proceeded to assail them with questions.

"Well, where have you been?" demanded the President. "Where have you been?" One by one he asked them when they went to bed the previous night. Next the President asked: "How many have written to their wives at least once a week since you've been down here?" There was a show of hands. "You had better check up because I have had several telegrams wanting to know what these fellows are doing."

R

RACIAL SUPERIORITY

We should realize that much of the trouble in the world
today is the result of false ideas of racial superiority.
—commencement address, Howard University, 1952
(see AMERICAN FAITH, CIVIL RIGHTS, COLOR LINE)

RAILROAD ROBBERY

Harry Truman wondered why an industry that in 1926
was handling 75 percent of the nation's traffic was skid-
ding toward bankruptcy a decade later. As chairman of
the Senate committee investigating the financial setup of
the railroads, Senator Truman uncovered corruption that
shocked and angered him. He called the railroad financiers "wrecking crews" and described certain Wall Street
lawyers as the "highest of the high hats" who pulled "tricks
that would make an ambulance chaser in a coroner's court
blush with shame."

In a speech to the Senate on June 3, 1937, Truman compared the railroad financiers to famous train robbers. "The first railroad robbery was committed on the Rock Island back in 1873 just east of Council Bluffs, Iowa. The man who committed that robbery used a gun and a horse and got up early in the morning. He and his gang took a chance of being killed and eventually most were. That railroad robber's name was Jesse James.

"The same Jesse James held up the Missouri Pacific in 1876 and took the paltry sum of seventeen thousand dollars from the express car. About thirty years after the Council Bluffs holdup, the Rock Island went through a looting by some gentlemen known as the 'Tin Plate Millionaires.' They used no guns but they ruined the railroad and got away with seventy million dollars or more. They did it by means of holding companies. Senators can see what 'pikers' Mr. James and his crowd were alongside of some real artists."

READING

Harry Truman was a voracious reader all his life. He claimed to have read all three thousand books in the Independence Public Library, including encyclopedias, by the time he was fourteen.

"I had no trouble sleeping," said Truman of his presidency. "I read myself to sleep every night in the White House, reading biography or the troubles of some President in the past."

Reading, his first diversion in life, was also his last. Forced in retirement to give up his morning walks, Harry Truman spent his last six years confined largely to the old house Bess's grandfather had built. In a letter to his niece Martha Anne Swoyer a year before his death, he wrote, "Reading is our best diversion these days."

No one ever loses by reading history, great literature—and even newspapers.

—*Autobiography*, 1980

Readers of good books, particularly books of biography and history, are preparing themselves for leadership. Not all readers become leaders. But all leaders must be readers.

—*Autobiography*, 1980
(see HISTORY)

RECESSION

Truman, explaining the difference between a recession and a depression, summed it up succinctly: "It's a recession when your neighbor loses his job; it's a depression when you lose your own."

RELIGION

"I've always believed that religion is something to live by and not talk about," Truman avowed. "Religious stuffed shirts are just as bad or worse than political ones in my opinion."

Truman's religion was very simple: "All the religion I have is found in the Ten Commandments and the Sermon on the Mount."

Truman did not care much for religious disputes, but if he had to bet on any group it would be the Baptists. "I myself always thought there were plenty of doors to heaven and don't think you have to go through any single one, although I thought the Baptist was most likely to get there."

(see CHURCH, PRAYER)

RELIGIOUS SECTS

Harry Truman liked to recount the story of how at age six he asked his grandfather what religious sect was best. His grandfather, Solomon Young, replied:

"All of them want to arrive at the same place, but they have to fight to see who has the inside track with Almighty. When a man spends Saturday night and Sunday doing too much howling and praying you had better go home and lock your smokehouse."

REPUBLICAN

"A sound government to the Republican," said Truman observing Eisenhower and Nixon at work, "is the kind of government where the president makes nice sounds while the vice-president snarls."

"If you can't convince them, confuse them."

> —Truman's description of the "Republican doctrine," Raleigh, October 19, 1948

(see FAIR PRICES)

REPUBLICAN PARTY

The Republican Party either corrupts its liberals or it expels them.

> —public papers, 1948

REPUBLICANS

"Republicans in Washington have a habit of becoming curiously deaf to the voice of the people," Truman charged at a campaign stop in Denver on September 20, 1948. "They have a hard time hearing what the ordinary people of the country are saying. But they have no trouble at all hearing what Wall Street is saying. They are able to catch the slightest whisper from big business and the special interests. . . .

"The Republicans have General Motors and General Electric and General Foods and General MacArthur . . . every general I know is on this list except general welfare."

The Republicans prefer to leave the power in the hands of the special interests rather than the man in the White House.
—Truman, "My First Eighty Years," 1964

The Republican party is the party of special privilege.
—Truman, "My First Eighty Years," 1964
(see MINIMUM WAGE)

RESIGNATION

All right, if that's the way you feel about it, I'll accept your resignation right now.
—Truman to Treasury Secretary Henry Morgenthau, July 5, 1945
(after Morgenthau said he would resign if he
could not go to the Potsdam conference)

REWARD

Since a child at my mother's knee, I have believed in honor, ethics, and right living as its own reward.
—written longhand in diary, 1931
(see HONOR)

RIDICULE

You must watch out for these people who make mountains out of something that doesn't exist—not even a molehill! . . . the best way to handle them is to *ridicule* them. You know, there's no stuffed shirt that can stand ridicule. When you stick a pin in that stuffed shirt and let the wind out, he's through!

—lecture, Columbia University, April 29, 1959
(see MCCARTHY, JOSEPH; MCCARTHYISM)

RIGHT

On his desk at the White House, President Truman kept a quotation from Mark Twain: "Always do right. This will gratify some people and astonish the rest."

What most people did not realize was how seriously Truman took this credo.

"If I think it is right, I am going to do it," he declared. "It makes no difference what the papers say if you are right."

I think the proper thing to do and the thing I have been doing, is to do what I think is right and let them all go to hell.

—letter to brother Vivian Truman, March 22, 1948

I think I've been right in the approach to all questions 90 percent of the time since I took over.

—diary, May 1, 1948

It is much better to go down fighting for what is right than to compromise your principles.

—memorandum, 1949

I shall continue to do what I think is right whether anybody likes it or not.

—memorandum, 1950

RIGHT HAS MIGHT

"Right Has Might" was the Trumanistic reply to the philosophy of Might Makes Right.

"We can no longer permit any nation, or group of nations, to attempt to settle their arguments with bombs and bayonets," he said in a radio broadcast in April 1945. "If we continue to abide by such decisions, we will be forced to accept the fundamental philosophy of our enemies, namely that 'Might Makes Right.' To deny this premise, and we most certainly do, we are obliged to provide the necessary means to refute it. Words are not enough. We must, once and for all, reverse the order, and prove by our acts conclusively, that Right Has Might. If we do not want to die together in war, we must learn to live together in peace."

ROGERS, WILL

"Almost a second Mark Twain," said Truman of the Oklahoman quarter-Cherokee humorist. "I'm glad his mother didn't believe in birth control."

When Will Rogers was killed in a plane crash in Alaska, Senator Truman was deeply saddened. "No one," he told his wife, "has done more to give us common sense."

ROOSEVELT, ELEANOR

On the fateful afternoon of April 12, 1945, Harry Truman found out that Mrs. Roosevelt wanted to speak with him.

Having concluded presiding over a Senate session, Vice-President Truman was about to "strike a liquid blow for liberty" with House Speaker Sam Rayburn when there was a call from the White House.

White House press secretary Stephen Early asked Truman to come over to the White House at once.

When Truman arrived he was ushered to Eleanor Roosevelt's second-floor study, where she was waiting for him.

Mrs. Roosevelt put her hand on his shoulder.

"Harry, the President is dead."

Truman was shocked. "Is there anything I can do for you?" he asked.

Mrs. Roosevelt shook her head. "Is there anything *we* can do for *you*? For you are the one in trouble now."

ROOSEVELT, FRANKLIN D.
(U.S. President 1933–1945)

After announcing the surrender of Japan on August 15, 1945, President Truman walked around the inside of the perimeter of the White House fence shaking hands with some of the thousands of deliriously happy Americans gathered outside the White House.

"The guns were silenced. The war was over. I was thinking of President Roosevelt, who had not lived to see this day. . . . I reached for the telephone and called Mrs. Roosevelt. I told her that in this hour of triumph I wished that it had been President Roosevelt, and not I, who had given the message to our people."

Truman first met President Roosevelt ("I was practically tongue-tied," he admitted later) in February 1935, a month after arriving in Washington as a freshman senator.

"He was a great executive, but he was not a good administrator. . . . I think Franklin Roosevelt did the very best he could under the circumstances, and the only thing I am sorry about is that his health failed and he didn't live until the end of his fourth term. . . .

"I always thought Franklin Roosevelt came nearer being the ideal president than anyone we'd had during my lifetime."

(see NEW DEAL)

ROOSEVELT, THEODORE
(U.S. President 1901–1909)

"Teddy Roosevelt was often more bull, without the moose, than substance," Truman wrote of the twenty-sixth president. "He made a great publicity stunt out of being a trust buster, but in fact he busted very few of them."

Truman recalled glimpsing Teddy Roosevelt as a boy.

"I was disappointed to find that he was no giant, but a little man in a long Prince Albert coat to make him look taller. After I became President I often thought back to that time. I found out that the people usually ran to see the President and not the man. A few decades back I had done exactly the same thing—running to see the President— who was then Teddy Roosevelt."

Nevertheless Truman admired Teddy Roosevelt's character, rating him his "second-favorite Republican," after Lincoln.

RUMORS

Rumors of Harry Truman's ill health were greatly exaggerated in December 1947. One night after reading of his rumored sickness in a newspaper, a "dangerously" well Harry Truman attached the news clipping to the following memorandum:

"I have just made some additions to my Kitchen Cabinet, which I will pass on to my successor in case the Cow should fall when she goes over the moon."

The appointments named to this Kitchen Cabinet included a Secretary for Inflation, a Secretary for Columnists, and a Secretary for Semantics.

"Then I have appointed a Secretary of Reaction. I want him to abolish flying machines and tell me how to restore oxcarts, oar boats and sailing ships. What a load he can take off my mind if he will put the atom back together so it cannot be broken up. What a worry that will abolish for both me and [Russian minister of foreign affairs] Vishinski."

RUSSIA

Russia is a great country and the Soviet Union is made up of sturdy people but they have been oppressed and downtrodden by dictatorships from the time of Ivan the Terrible and Peter the Great to this very day. Sometime, and I hope this is the beginning of that time, the Russian people will awaken to the meaning of liberty and world peace and the world can live happily ever after.

—diary, Salzburg, June 4, 1956

RUSSIANS

"I went to Potsdam with the kindliest feelings toward Russia—in a year and a half they cured me of it," Truman wrote to his daughter Margaret on March 3, 1948.

"They are tough bargainers and always ask for the whole earth, expecting maybe to get an acre."

And anyway the Russians need us more than we need them.

—*Memoirs, Vol. 1*, 1955

S

SCIENCE

Our science and industry owe their strength to the spirit of free inquiry and the spirit of free enterprise that character-ize our country.

—letter to Senator Brien McMahon, February 1, 1946

SENATE

When Harry Truman first arrived in the Senate, he felt "as timid as a country boy arriving on the campus of a great university for his first year."

At first he was modest, describing himself as "only a humble member of the next Senate, green as grass and ignorant as a fool about practically everything worth knowing."

But he remembered some advice given him by an old judge.

"There was an old county judge who was with me on

the county court in Jackson County, and he gave me some advice before I left Independence to come to Washington."

The judge, who once worked for a Mississippi senator in Washington, had said, " 'Harry, don't you go to the Senate with an inferiority complex. You sit there about six months, and you wonder how you got there. But after that, you'll wonder how the rest of them got there.' "

There are liars, trimmers, and pussyfooters on both sides of the aisle in the Senate and the House.

—diary, November 30, 1950

SENATOR

Asked for his advice to a senator aspiring to higher office, President Truman suggested:

"Be very shy and aloof, say you want to go home and write your memoirs. Say you would not touch the crown with a ten-foot pole—refuse it at least thrice—but say nothing about just taking it in hand and wearing it at the proper time. This method may bring home the bacon."

(see VICE-PRESIDENT)

SENIOR CITIZEN

I don't like ... to be called a "senior citizen." I still get around and when I get to be a "senior citizen" I hope they will put me in a pine box and cover me up.

—letter to former chief administrative assistant Edward McKim, October 15, 1963

SHORTEST SPEECH

The Mayor of Independence, an old friend of Truman's, introduced him once to a crowd by saying only, "Ladies and gentlemen, the President of the United States."

To which Truman responded: "That was the shortest speech I ever heard you make in all my life. I appreciate that and I know you meant every word of it."

SLEEPING PILL

Harry Truman was a sound sleeper and proud of it, boasting, "I've been one of the worst customers the sleeping pill manufacturers ever had."

SMALL BUSINESS

"I think small business, the small farmer, the small corporations are the backbone of any free society," President Truman wrote to a corporate leader after the war, "and when there are too many people on relief and too few people at the top who control the wealth of the country we must look out."

SNOBBERY

"I am sorry to see a growth of snobbery in the United States in recent years," Truman commented in retirement. "I especially deplore the tendency to look down on people who work with their hands."

S.O.B.

Harry Truman caused a great uproar with his use of the abbreviation "s.o.b.," an expression forbidden in the movies at that time. As H. L. Mencken chronicles this linguistic development in *The American Language*: "When Harry S. Truman used the abbreviated form [s.o.b.] in a letter from the White House, to a music critic who had spoken disparagingly of daughter Margaret's singing, the public reaction was only slightly less violent than if General Douglas MacArthur had been discovered to be a paid agent of the Kremlin."

Years later, after leaving the White House, the Trumans visited San Francisco. They were on their way to dinner at the house of George Killion, head of the steamship company on whose liner they were to travel to Hawaii.

The chauffeur got them in the right neighborhood, but had the address wrong.

Truman went to the door and rang the bell. "An unmistakably Republican-looking gentleman" (as he put it later) opened the door.

The gentleman did not know where the Killions lived, and added, "By the way, I hope I'm not hurting your feelings but you look exactly like that old s.o.b. Harry Truman."

"I hope I'm not hurting your feelings either," Truman replied. "But I *am* that old s.o.b. Harry Truman."

SOCIAL LEADERS

Every time one of those great dinners comes up, you can only seat ninety-nine people in the State Dining Room in the White House, and you know what a time it is to get those ninety-nine places filled . . . without making some of the great old social leaders feel pretty bad because they're not on the list. But sometimes it does them good to be left off; they behave a little better after that.

—Columbia University, April 27, 1957

SOCIALISM

President Truman defended his domestic programs against charges of "socialism": "They keep yapping about 'socialism' and a lot of other silly slogans to try and stop every measure for the good of the people."

(see HEALTH INSURANCE)

142

SPECIAL PRIVILEGE

"It hasn't been easy to make the New Deal and the Fair Deal a success," said President Truman in his second term. "We have had a lot of opposition. Sometimes representatives of special privilege have been able to hold us back . . .

"Most of the special privilege boys are better off than they have ever been in their lives, but they still say that the New Deal and the Fair Deal are taking the country to the dogs and to ruin . . ."

Truman concluded: "It's a wonderful ruin, and I'm glad to be a part of it."

(see NEW DEAL)

SPEECHES

"Well, the speech seems to have made a hit according to all the papers," remarked Truman, who, like most self-motivated individuals, was often his own worst critic. "Shows you never can tell. I thought it was rotten."

I heard a fellow tell a story about how he felt when he had to make speeches. He said when he has to make a speech, he felt like the fellow who was at the funeral of his wife, and the undertaker had asked him if he would ride down to the cemetery in the same car with his mother-in-law. He said, "Well, I can do it, but it's just going to spoil the whole day for me."

—campaign remarks, Dexter, Iowa, September 18, 1948
(see PUBLIC SPEAKING)

SQUIRREL HEAD

A reporter asked the President if he'd called a certain general a "squirrel head" as rumored.

The President said he hadn't, and looked to his wife for confirmation.

She raised one eyebrow. "Really?" she said. "It sounds just like you."

STALIN, JOSEPH

During the Potsdam conference, Truman received a secret report informing him that the first successful atomic test had been completed in New Mexico. Soon afterward Truman met privately with Soviet premier Joseph Stalin and told him the United States had a superbomb in production.

Stalin did not blink or seem surprised. He was glad to hear of this weapon, he said, and hoped it would be put to good use against the Japanese.

"When I told Stalin about the atom bomb," Truman recalled later, "he merely shrugged his shoulders, as though he knew the secret all the time . . . which the son of a bitch probably did."

STATE FAIR

"I don't mind being an exhibit here myself," President Truman confided to the crowd at the North Carolina State Fair in Raleigh on October 19, 1948. "I think I belong right here. I'm a home-grown American farm product."

STATESMAN

"Some people suggest that you are getting mellowed and less militant. Is that so?" asked a student.

"Not in the slightest degree," replied the former president. "They are trying to make an elder statesman of me, but they will never succeed."

A statesman is a politician who's been dead ten or fifteen years.

—quoted in the *New York World-Telegram & Sun*, April 12, 1958

STATESMANSHIP

"Where poverty goes in the front door, love goes out the transom," Vice-President Barkley remarked at one of President Truman's cabinet meetings.

To which, Barkley recalled later, President Truman added:

"And where politics goes in the front door, statesmanship flies out the transom."

STEVENSON, ADLAI

President Truman, after announcing he would not run again, urged Adlai Stevenson III, governor of Illinois, to run against Eisenhower in 1952. When they met at Blair House, Truman reportedly said, "Adlai, if a knucklehead like me can be president and not do too badly, think what a really educated smart guy like you could do in the job."

Stevenson said no at first, later changed his mind, and subsequently ran a faltering campaign. "What am I doing wrong?" he asked Harry Truman once when they were alone.

Truman walked to the window and pointed to a man standing across the street from their hotel. "The thing you have got to do is to learn how to reach that man."

It was Truman's way of telling Stevenson he must learn to communicate with the man on the street.

STUDENTS

"I always tell students that it is what you learn after you know it all that counts."

Truman, always a voracious reader, set an example to

students of a lifelong learner. "I always tell the students who write to me, to obtain all of the education that they can possibly get and to read as many good books as they can."

(see READING)

STUFFED SHIRT

Harry Truman had little patience for "stuffed shirts." "There's nothing in the world I dislike more than a stuffed shirt who tries to put on a front and make people think he's something that he isn't."

(see PRIMA DONNAS)

SUPREME COURT

Whenever you put a man on the Supreme Court, he ceases to be your friend, you can be sure of that.

—Columbia University, April 28, 1959

SWEARING

President Truman once exploded in anger at an officer's club press conference. "Everybody is telling me who I should have on my staff and in my Cabinet!" he exclaimed. "No s.o.b. is going to dictate to me who I'm going to have!"

Bess Truman blushed when she heard this indelicate language, and the President was criticized by her and others for using it. A Washington rector came to the President's defense, saying that under similar provocation he might have said the same thing. Informed of the rector's remark, President Truman quipped, "I just wish that rector would go talk to my wife!"

(see S.O.B.)

SWEDE STORY

Cheering up a friend who had fallen off a roof and was still recuperating, Harry wrote:

"I notice at the end of your letter, you fell off the roof while nailing on some shingles. It brought up a story ... about a Swede who had the same experience.

"This Swede was in Alaska as a prospector, used up his supplies and started for Dawson City. A blizzard caught him and he stopped at the first house. Only the woman of the place was at home. He asked if he could stay the night. She gave him permission to stay.

"He had a lot of blankets with him and when she came down and told him she was cold, he gave her another blanket.

"Went on to Dawson the next day, and then to the United States and began following his trade as a carpenter. He was nailing shingles on a roof—fell off and broke his leg.

"When asked how it happened, he said he 'ves tinkin' about what 'dot woman wanted' in Alaska. It occurred to him and he said, 'I tried to kick myself in the behind, fell off de roof and broke the leg.' "

T

TAFT, WILLIAM HOWARD
(U.S. President 1909–1913)

"A fat, jolly, likable, mediocre man."

This is how Harry Truman tersely described William Howard Taft, the twenty-seventh President.

TAXES

Nobody likes to pay taxes—a man will cry his head off over paying $100 taxes on his income, but he will go out and throw away $500 or $1000 on a poker game and say nothing about it. I guess that is the way the human animal is made.

> —letter to Stanley Marcus (owner of a Dallas Neiman-Marcus store who complained to Truman), July 12, 1949

While I fought for a more equal distribution of the nation's prosperity among all its citizens, I never advocated taxing the rich to pay the poor. The rate of taxation, to be fair, must be based on ability to pay.

—*Memoirs, Vol. 2*, 1956

TAYLOR, ZACHARY
(U.S. President 1849–1850)

Truman had this to say about the twelfth president, Zachary Taylor, a military hero of the Mexican War elected on his record as a soldier:

"I can't be charitable and say that he failed to carry out his program; he didn't have any program to carry out."

TEACHER

"If I hadn't got into this other business, I might have turned out to be a teacher," Truman confided to Merle Miller, "and if I do say so, I don't think I would have been so bad at it."

It makes not much difference what sort of building you're in when you're after knowledge, but it does count entirely on who teaches you.

—letter to cousin Nellie Noland, October 29, 1949
(see STUDENTS)

TELEVISION

On October 5, 1947, Harry Truman became the first President to address the nation from the White House on television. He used that opportunity to call on Americans to save food for Europe by observing meatless Tuesdays and eggless Thursdays.

"A man is never quite himself on a television program," said Truman, who was not as comfortable with the visual medium as future presidents would have to be. "He can only be himself when he personally meets people face to face. . . . he has to be just himself without the benefit of makeup."

TERM LIMITS

President Truman decided not to run for a third term. He wrote his decision in a memorandum dated April 16, 1950:

> Washington, Jefferson, Monroe, Madison, Andrew Jackson and Woodrow Wilson, as well as Calvin Coolidge, stood by the precedent of two terms. Only Grant, Theodore Roosevelt and F.D.R. made the attempt to break that precedent. F.D.R. succeeded.
>
> In my opinion eight years as President is enough and sometimes too much for any man to serve in that capacity.
>
> There is a lure in power. It can get into a man's blood just as gambling and lust for money have been known to do.
>
> I know I could be elected again and continue to break the old precedent as it was broken by F.D.R. It should not be done.

President Truman locked up the memorandum in his desk and kept his decision secret until he made a surprise announcement on March 29, 1952, at the Jefferson-Jackson Day Dinner in the National Guard Armory in Washington, D.C.

"I shall not be a candidate for re-election. I have served my country long, and I think efficiently and honestly. I shall not accept a renomination. I do not feel that it is my duty to spend another four years in the White House."

Even without a third term, Harry Truman was president for nearly two full terms—seven years, nine months, or to be precise, 2,841 days.

TERRIBLE CONGRESSMAN

Harry Truman called the Republican-dominated 80th Congress "the worst we've ever had" and singled out one "terrible congressman" in particular—Bertrand Gearheart.

"You have got a terrible Congressman here in this district," President Truman told a Fresno crowd at a California campaign stop on September 23, 1948.

"He is one of the worst," Truman berated Gearheart. "He is one of the worst obstructionists in the Congress. He has done everything he possibly could to cut the throats of the farmer and the laboring man. If you send him back, that will be your fault if you get your own throat cut."

Harry Truman liked to talk tough like this. He liked to let the opposition know which side he was on.

"I am speaking plainly these days," he said. "I am telling you facts. Nobody else will tell 'em to you. . . ."

THINK

I have never forced myself to think when my energy was low. I simply will not tackle a problem involving an important decision until I feel completely relaxed.

—*Mr. Citizen*, 1960
(see DECISIONMAKING)

THIRTY-SECOND

Harry Truman was officially the thirty-third president. As a matter of personal conviction, he felt he was only the *thirty-second* president.

"I am the thirty-second man to be President. If you count the administrations of Grover Cleveland twice because another President held office between Cleveland's first and second terms, you might try to justify the designation of me as thirty-third President. But then why don't you number all the second terms of other Presidents and the third and fourth terms of President Roosevelt, and where will you be? I am the thirty-second President."

THOUGHT CONTROL

Vetoing the Internal Security Act of 1950, President Truman charged Congress with an un-American "frenzy" of Communist "witchhunting."

The bill, said Truman, "is so contrary to our national interests that it would actually put the Government into the business of thought control, by requiring the deportation of any alien who distributes or publishes, or who is affiliated with an organization which distributes or publishes, any written or printed matter advocating [or merely expressing belief in] the economic and governmental doctrines of any form of totalitarianism. . . .

"Thus, the Attorney General would be required to deport any alien operating or connected with a well-stocked bookshop containing books on economics or politics. . . .

"There should be no room in our laws for such hysterical provisions. The next logical step would be to 'burn the books.' "

Truman's veto was overridden by Congress on September 23, 1950. "One of the bad results of the act soon came to pass," he wrote in his *Memoirs*. "The Communists now began to scurry underground."

(see EDUCATION, FREEDOM OF EXPRESSION)

TOP DOG

President Truman submitted his civil rights program to Congress on February 2, 1948. Off the record, he said: "The top dog in a world which is 90 percent colored ought to clean his own house."

(see CIVIL RIGHTS, UNDERDOG)

TREASURER

A frustrated former President Truman wrote the following letter to the Treasurer of the United States:

December 26, 1961

Dear Sir:
I'd appreciate it if you could find a way to place debits and credits so an ordinary citizen like myself could understand what you are trying to show.

Why don't you set up yours so any citizen who understands debit from credit can know what you are doing? I don't think that the financial advisor of God Himself would be able to understand what the financial position of the United States government is, by reading your statement.

Harry Truman

TRICKLE DOWN

The Republican policy is to let the big fellow get the big incomes, and let a little of it trickle down off the table like the crumbs fell to Lazarus.

—speech, Merced, California, September 23, 1948
(see REPUBLICAN)

TROUBLE

A year from now I'm going to be right back in the same trouble I'm in now.

—banquet speech, Palmer House, Chicago, June 1948

TRUMAN, BESS WALLACE

Harry Truman first laid admiring eyes upon Bess Truman in a Sunday school class—"a very beautiful little lady with lovely blue eyes and the prettiest golden curls I've ever seen."

It turned out to be one Elizabeth Virginia "Bessie" Wallace.

"I was smitten at once," Truman recalled decades later, "and still am." (Even in his sixties Truman referred to her as his "sweetheart.")

"Bessie" was the girl of his dreams from fifth grade on.

"From the fifth grade in school, which was taught by her Aunt Nannie, until I graduated from high school we were in the same classes. If I succeeded in carrying her books to school or back home for her I had a big day."

Harry Truman proposed many times to Bess before she finally accepted in 1917, when she was thirty-three and he was thirty-four. They postponed their wedding when he enlisted in the Army to fight in World War I. "I didn't think it was right to get married and come home a cripple and have the most beautiful and sweetest girl in the world tied down."

Harry Truman returned from France on April 20, 1919, and married "Bess" Elizabeth Virginia Wallace on June 28, 1919. They were married for fifty-three years.

"You know, I went to Sunday school right across there," said President Truman at a dedication ceremony on November 6, 1950, in Independence, unveiling a replica of the Liberty Bell.

"And in that Sunday school class I met a little blue-eyed, golden-haired girl—my first sweetheart. Her eyes are still blue, but her hair is no longer golden; it's silver, like mine. And she is still my sweetheart."

Bess Truman was criticized sometimes for not coloring her hair or wearing heavy makeup, like other Washington society ladies. Truman defended his wife, saying: "She looks exactly as a woman her age should look."

When an aide told Truman about the "Gentlemen Prefer

Blondes" billboard ad, the president shook his head and said, "Real gentlemen prefer gray."

One Christmas he came upon Bess burning letters he had written to her.

"You shouldn't be doing that!"

"Why not? I've read them several times," said Bess.

"But think of history," pleaded Harry.

She answered, "I have."

TRUMAN, MARGARET

President Truman attended one of his daughter's singing concerts in Washington, sitting in a prominent box with her voice coach. As the program was about to begin, Harry Truman appeared to be more nervous than Margaret (the first daughter of a President ever to attempt a professional career of her own).

"Don't pay any attention to me when I start to tear up the program," Truman said to the voice coach. "I always do that when I'm nervous."

"I do the same thing," admitted the voice coach.

Between them they tore up four programs that evening, and Margaret sang three encores. Later in life she became a bestselling author of biographies and mystery novels.

The vast majority of our people can never understand what a terrible handicap it is to a lovely girl to have her father the president of the United States.

> —letter to Barbara Heggie (writer of "What Makes Margaret Sing?" *Women's Home Companion*), December 20, 1950
>
> (see COLLEGE)

TRUMAN, MARTHA

Harry Truman's mother had faith in her son from the beginning. "I knew that boy would amount to something," she told reporters when he was elected to the Senate. "He could plow the straightest row of corn in the county."

Martha Truman raised her son to "be good," and his scrupulousness once cost her $11,000. When one of the county's new roads cut eleven acres from her property, he felt he must deny her the usual reimbursement from the county of $1,000 an acre, as a matter of principle, because he was presiding judge of Jackson County and she was his mother. She was furious at him.

After Harry Truman was sworn in as President, Martha Truman commented to the press: "I can't really be glad he is president because I'm sorry that President Roosevelt is dead. If he had been voted in, I would be out waving a flag, but it doesn't seem right to be very happy or wave a flag now."

Reading his mother's statement reprinted in the papers, Truman was pleased. "If it had been prepared by the best public relations man it could not have been better."

Truman discovered that his mother "did not seem to feel that there was anything special about my being in the White House or my being president. She thought it was just the natural thing."

(see MOTHER)

TRUTH

You can disagree all you want on any subject, farm, labor, monetary, debt control or foreign policy and I won't care at all—if, if you tell the truth.

—letter to Arthur Krock, September 11, 1952
(see BIG LIE)

TWAIN, MARK

Harry Truman liked to quote Mark Twain's remark, "If we had less statesmanship, we could get along with fewer battleships," and other Twainisms.

On his desk at the White House Truman kept as a memento a plaque with Mark Twain's words: "Always be good. This will gratify some people and astonish the rest."

Truman wrote in reflection: "I wonder if it may not be such simple characters as Tom Sawyer and Huckleberry Finn who will, as symbols, show the world our undying contribution to the civilization on our continent. . . ."

(see HUMOR, RIGHT, WRITING)

TYLER, JOHN
(U.S. President 1841–1845)

Truman had this to say about the tenth American president, John Tyler:

"He was a contrary old son of a bitch."

U

ULCER PAY

President Roosevelt's press secretary, Steve Early, stayed on in the Truman administration, working at the Pentagon. No longer the President's daily spokesman, Steve Early still worried about the President. Truman told White House reporters:

"I received a card the other day from Steve Early which said, 'Don't Worry Me—I am an 8 Ulcer Man on 4 Ulcer Pay.' "

(see WORRY)

UN-AMERICAN

I have said many a time that I think the Un-American Activities Committee in the House of Representatives was the most un-American thing in America.

—Columbia University, April 29, 1959
(see MCCARTHY, JOSEPH; MCCARTHYISM)

UNCLOTHED

During a whistle-stop tour, Truman's train arrived very late one night in Missoula, Montana. A small crowd of local residents were still waiting for the President at the station, hoping he would appear on the rear platform. When Harry Truman did appear, he was wearing pajamas and a bathrobe. "I am sorry I had gone to bed," he told the patient Montanans. "But I thought you would like to see what I look like, even if I didn't have on any clothes."

(see CLOTHES)

UNDERDOG

Sympathy for the underdog did not blind Truman to the dangers of underdoggery-turned-demagoguery.

"I was never for the underdog, in turn, becoming the top dog with complete power to act. When the underdog gets power, he too often turns out to be an even more brutal top dog."

(see TOP DOG)

UNITED NATIONS

President Truman hosted a diplomatic reception at his hotel before addressing the United Nations founding conference in San Francisco in 1945.

The President was disappointed to see that the only refreshment furnished by the State Department was a bowl of amber fluid diplomatically called "champagne punch."

"Hell, that stuff will rust your pipes!" Truman gestured to the foreign ministers, ambassadors, and VIPs around him. "Come on up to my suite, gentlemen, and I'll pour you a real drink!"

There was a moment of shocked silence, then broad

grins broke out, and a crowd followed the President to the elevators.

If the United Nations yields to the forces of aggression, no nation will be safe or secure.

—press conference, November 30, 1950
(see KOREA)

UNITED STATES

The United States was created by the boys and girls who could not get along at home.

—memorandum, June 7, 1945

UNUSUAL PROCEDURE

"As always, I am just trying to do the job I am supposed to do," President Truman responded to a criticism of his "unusual procedures," "and a lot of times, in public service, that is an unusual procedure."

USUAL ASS

After a bad review in the *Chicago Tribune* for a State of the Union address, President Truman recalled Lincoln's bad notices after the Gettysburg Address. "In 1864 the Chicago *Tribune* printed the full text of Lincoln's speech at Gettysburg with the comment that the President had made the 'usual ass of himself.' Believe me, it is flattering to be put in such company."

VAN BUREN, MARTIN
(U.S. President 1837–1841)

The eighth president was Martin Van Buren, of whom Harry Truman said simply: "I've got to say that our country would have done just as well not to have had Van Buren as president."

(see PRESIDENTS)

VETO

President Truman vetoed the Republican-sponsored Basing Point Bill of 1950 (setting freight charges affecting the price of steel), as he said he would. Asked if it had been a difficult decision, he answered:

"I intended to veto it all along. In fact, I feel like the blacksmith on the Missouri jury. The judge asked if he was prejudiced against the defendant. 'Oh no, Judge,' he said. 'I think we ought to give him a fair trial. Then I think we ought to take the s.o.b. out and string him up.' "

VICE-PRESIDENT

"There's an old joke that the vice-president's principal chore is to get up in the morning and ask how the president is feeling."

Harry Truman joked with the press about the idleness of the second-highest office in the land, not knowing how few his days as Vice-President were numbered.

A reporter accidentally called Truman "Mr. President" at a Senate press conference on April 11, 1945, to which Truman replied:

"Boys, those are fighting words out in Missouri where I come from. You'd better smile when you say that! You know right here is where I've always wanted to be, and the only place I ever wanted to be. The Senate—that's just my speed and my style.

"I did what I could. I did my best. I was getting along fine, until I stuck my neck out too far and got too famous. And then they made me VP and now I can't do anything."

This press conference turned out to be Truman's last as Vice-President. The following day, April 12, 1945, Franklin D. Roosevelt died of a stroke and Harry Truman was sworn in as President, less than three months after being sworn in as Vice-President.

(see SENATE)

VICTORY

"I've been in many and many election campaigns as you people here in Missouri know," Truman mused after his victory over Dewey in 1948. "After the election's over I bear no malice or feel badly toward anyone because the fellow who lost feels badly enough without eating crow."

VOLCANO

On a goodwill tour of Mexico, President Truman was asked by Mexican President Alemán what he thought of the Paricutín volcano.

"Frankly," Truman replied, "it's nothing compared to the one I'm sitting on in Washington."

VOTES

By their votes ye shall know them.
—speech, Los Angeles, September 23, 1948

WALKING

Walking was Harry Truman's favorite form of exercise, especially after age fifty. "After you are fifty years old," he wrote, "it is the best exercise you can take. Of course, some aging exhibitionists try to prove that they can play tennis or handball or anything they did when they were eighteen. And every once in a while one of them falls dead of a heart attack. I say that's not for me."

When Truman said walking he meant walking—not strolling, sauntering, lumbering, or loitering. He was a brisk walker who put the press on notice that they would be hard-pressed to keep up with him.

Merriman Smith, one of the White House reporters, suspected the morning walks were a publicity gimmick at first. After two weeks of daily dawn "constitutionals" (as the President called his early-morning walks) Smith concluded that Truman actually liked getting up early and exercising "at a pace normally reserved for track stars."

President Truman's peripatetic press conferences were

one of the distinctive hallmarks of the Truman administration.

"It might be interesting to you to know," the retiring President said to reporters on January 15, 1953, "that since 1945, when I came up here to the White House, I have taken a thousand and two morning walks. Some of you went on one or two, but you didn't go on any more. . . ."

(see EARLY, HIGH HEELS)

WAR

It all seems to have been in vain. Memories are short and appetites for power and glory are insatiable. Old tyrants depart. New ones take their place. Old allies become the foe. The recent enemy becomes the friend. It is all very baffling and trying, [but] we cannot lose hope, we cannot despair. For it is all too obvious that if we do not abolish war on this earth, then surely, one day, war will abolish us from the earth.

—remarks, Independence, Missouri, January 25, 1966
(see PEACE)

WAR PREVENTION

The one purpose that dominated me in everything I thought and did [as President] was to prevent a third world war.

—Memoirs, Vol. 2, 1956

Warfare, no matter what weapons it employs, is a means to an end, and if that end can be achieved by negotiated settlements of conditional surrender, there is no need for war.

—Memoirs, Vol. 1, 1955

I have always been opposed even to the thought of fighting a "preventive war." There is nothing more foolish than to think that war can be stopped by war. You don't "prevent" anything by war except peace.

—*Memoirs, Vol. 2,* 1956

WARS

Victorious nations cannot, on the surrender of a vicious and dangerous enemy, turn their backs and go home. Wars are different from baseball games, where, at the end of the game, the teams get dressed and leave the park.

—public papers, 1947

WASHINGTON, D.C.

"If you want a friend in Washington, buy a dog," Truman advised. "There are more prima donnas per square foot in public life here in Washington than in all the opera companies ever to exist."

(see PRIMA DONNAS)

WASHINGTON, GEORGE
(U.S. President 1789–1797)

Truman rated George Washington the greatest of presidents. "George Washington was the best administrator this country ever had, and I say this acknowledging that the scope and problems of government have increased hundred-fold since Washington's time."

Washington was not perfect, certainly. "He was a pompous man in some ways. When he went to state affairs, for example, he wore velvet and satin and diamond knee-buckles and powdered his hair."

But Washington made presidential decisions without precedent. "When the decisions were hard to make, he made them, and he carried them through."

In his State of the Union address in 1952, President Truman invoked Washington.

> In that darkest of all winters in American history, at Valley Forge, George Washington said: "We must not, in so great a contest, expect to meet with nothing but sunshine." With that spirit they won their fight for freedom. We must have that same faith and vision. In the great contest in which we are engaged today we cannot expect to have fair weather all the way. But it is a contest just as important for this country and for all men as the desperate struggle that George Washington fought through to victory.
>
> (see PRESIDENTS' RATINGS)

WASHINGTON RENTS

Newly elected Missouri senator Harry Truman went to Washington in late 1934 to scout out the nation's capital, where he would reside for the next six years. After returning safely to Missouri, he spoke at the Kansas City Elks Club about Washington's notoriously high rents.

"My trouble is that I probably won't find a place to live. You see, I have to live on my salary, and a cubbyhole rents for a hundred and fifty dollars a month there."

WATERMELON SEEDS

The Trumans were not as formal or reserved as the Roosevelts. So the White House staffers found out in 1945 soon after the Trumans moved in.

One night during dinner President Truman, without warning, flipped a watermelon seed at the First Lady.

The First Lady, unable to endure such an assault on her dignity without retaliation, returned fire.

Soon watermelon seeds were airborne in all directions. Not even the butler who came to clear the table was spared pelting.

The other servants did not mind much. They howled with laughter as the Trumans joined forces to bombard the butler with watermelon seeds.

WEBSTER, DANIEL

Truman described the famed orator Daniel Webster as:

"A windbag. He made a great many orations, and I imagine he did a very good job, but he was still a windbag."

WEIGHT

My good doctor is all the time trying to cut my weight down. Of course he's right and I should weigh 170 pounds. Now I weigh 175. What's five pounds between my doctor and me?

When I moved into the White House I went up to 185. I've now hit an average of 175. I walk two miles most every morning at a hundred and twenty eight steps a minute, I eat no bread but one piece of toast at breakfast, no butter, no sugar, no sweets. Usually have fruit, one egg, a strip of bacon and half a glass of skimmed milk for breakfast; liver and bacon or sweet breads or ham or fish and spinach and another nonfattening vegetable for lunch with fruit for dessert. For dinner I have a fruit cup, steak, a couple of nonfattening vegetables and an ice, orange, pineapple or raspberry for dinner. So—I maintain my waist line and can wear suits bought in 1935.

—diary, January 3, 1953
(see DIETS)

WELL-MEANING

"About the meanest thing you can say about a man," said Harry Truman of a well-meaning man, "is that he means well."

WHISTLE-STOP

During the 1948 "whistle-stop" campaign, Truman traveled nearly 32,000 miles by rail and gave 356 speeches, usually from the train's rear platform.

At the end of the speech Truman would say, "How'd ja like to meet the family?"

Bess Truman would step through a curtain to join Harry on the rear platform. He would wink at the crowd and introduce her as "the Boss." Then he would introduce "the one who bosses the Boss" as Margaret stepped through the curtain.

The train would begin to pull away with the Trumans standing on the rear platform waving goodbye to the receding crowd.

WHITE HOUSE

"The White House is a difficult place to raise a family, and the environment is not always a normal atmosphere for an American child," Truman related. "It seems that there's somebody for supper every night."

As he was packing up to leave the White House in January 1953, Truman told reporters, "If I had known there would be so much work leaving this place, I'd have run again."

WHITNEY, AL

"You can't make a president out of a ribbon clerk," was what Al Whitney, head of the trainmen's union, said of President Truman.

Whitney was responding to harsh words from Truman, who was resisting a railroad strike in 1946.

A year later Whitney made an appointment to see the President. Whitney walked twice around the White House, working up his nerve. When he stepped into the Oval Office, Truman greeted him with an outstretched hand.

"It's good to see you, Al. Let's not waste time discussing the past. Let's just agree we both received bad advice."

"Mr. President," said Whitney, "I'm a third-generation Irishman who's part Scotch and you know they are kind of hotheaded sometimes."

Truman nodded and said, "I'm made up on the same plan."

WIFE

"When a man gets the right kind of wife, his career is made," Harry Truman liked to say, "—and I got just that."

(see also TRUMAN, BESS; WOMEN)

WILSON, WOODROW
(U.S. President 1913–1921)

"Woodrow Wilson served as a constant example to me of how to operate and function as president of the United States," Truman wrote in tribute to the twenty-eighth president, under whose portrait he took the oath of office on April 12, 1945.

"Wilson had the idea that he was *the* smartest man in the United States . . . of course people associated with him didn't like that attitude, but it's probably the truth."

Truman conceded that Wilson was not the funniest of presidents. "He wanted almost desperately to help people and improve the world around him, but he was no bundle of laughs. . . .

"But Wilson had a sense of humor, too, and because he had a thin face and wore glasses from the age of eight and considered himself an ugly man, he once wrote a limerick about himself that I still hear people quoting from time to time . . .

For beauty I am not a star
There are others more handsome by far
But my face I don't mind it
For I am behind it
It's the people in front that I jar."

WINCHELL, WALTER

One of Harry Truman's least favorite human beings was
Walter Winchell, an often critical news correspondent
whom he called a "newsliar," of whom he wrote:

"If Winchell ever told the truth it was by accident and
not intentional."

WINDY

"Is it as windy in Independence as it is in Washington?" a
reporter asked Truman during a visit to the National Press
Club on May 10, 1954, a very windy day.

Truman replied: "It is when I'm there."

WOMEN

"Three things can ruin a man—money, power, and women,"
Harry Truman liked to say. "I never had any money, I never
wanted power, and the only woman in my life is up at the
house right now."

When an Army PR man had the temerity to ask the
President if there was anything he wanted—*women*, for
example—to let him know, Truman cut him off sharply.

"Listen son, I married my sweetheart. She doesn't run
around on me, and I don't run around on her. I want that
understood. Don't ever mention that kind of stuff to me
again."

WOMEN PRESIDENTS

"I've said for a long time that women have everything else, they might as well have the presidency." This was Harry Truman's standard reply to the standard question of women presidents.

"We are almost a matriarchy now. The women control the finances of the country. They could do it. There isn't any doubt but what a woman would make a good President. They make good Senators, good members of the House of Representatives and have held other important offices in the Government of the United States."

WORK

It takes work to do anything well. Most people expect everything and do nothing to get it. . . . It just takes work and more work to accomplish anything—and your dad knows it better than anyone.

—letter to Margaret Truman, November 24, 1937

WORLD WAR III

"Foreign policy has been costly," acknowledged President Truman. "But World War III would be ten times as costly."

(SEE FOREIGN POLICY, MARSHALL PLAN, PEACE)

WORRY

There are worriers and there are nonworriers. Truman was one of the latter.

"I walk and swim and worry very little," Truman confessed. "I appoint people to responsible positions to worry for me. You have no idea how satisfactory that policy is."

Truman was more of a mental warrior than a worrier.

"All my life I've been relatively free from worry, and maybe that's the best formula for long life."

(see DECISIONMAKING, ULCER PAY)

WRINKLES

When a woman in a crowd during a 1948 campaign "whistle-stop" commented on his "dimples," Truman corrected her:

"Not dimples, they're wrinkles. You can't have dimples at sixty-four."

"If you call those wrinkles," the woman retorted, "then you are too old."

The President replied, "Now you're speaking for yourself."

WRITING

During his second term in office, President Truman, like most of his predecessors, was disappointed with what was written about him by the writers of the free press. He made this sterling vow: "I am going to spend the rest of my life in an endeavor to cause a return to truthful writing and reporting."

Truman spent much of his retirement writing his memoirs. When criticized for his writing style, he vehemently denied having any.

"We have had some excellent writers of simple English in this country. Mark Twain's *Tom Sawyer* is an outstanding example of the simplest way to say things so that people can understand them. If I were going to cultivate a style of writing, I would try to make it as simple as possible and straightforward, and state the facts as they are. . . . But as for style in speaking or writing, I never had any."

(see ORATORS; TWAIN, MARK)

Y

YES MAN

A yes-man on the White House staff or in the cabinet is worthless!

—*Memoirs, Vol. 2,* 1956

YOUNG PEOPLE

This Republic of ours is unique in the history of government and if the young people coming along in the future generations do not understand it and appreciate what they have it will go the way of the Judges of Israel, the City of Greece, the great Roman Republic and the Dutch Republic.

These young people must understand that our great Government was obtained by "blood, sweat and tears" and a thousand years of effort on the part of the great thinkers over that period and blood-letting revolutions and sacrifices by the people.

—letter to Stanley Whiteway (a contributor to the Truman Library), January 21, 1959

YOUNG, SOLOMON

During the 1944 vice-presidential campaign, rumors were spread by certain opposing parties that Harry S. Truman was Jewish, since his grandfather's name was Solomon. In rural Missouri the Ku Klux Klan distributed thousands of imitation ballots in which his name was printed as "Harry Solomon Truman."

"I am not Jewish," Truman responded, "but if I were I would not be ashamed of it."

(see RELIGIOUS SECTS)

Z

ZEROES

Disappointed that only two hundred people showed up for a major speech in Jacksonville, Florida, in 1946, President Truman wrote his daughter Margaret:

"The optimistic national committee man and committee woman assured me there'd be two thousand—but zeroes are easy to put on in politics."

A BRIEF BIOGRAPHY OF
HARRY S. TRUMAN

Harry S. Truman is born May 8, 1884, at home in Lamar, Missouri.

~1884–1888~

My first memory is that of chasing a frog around the back yard in Cass County, Missouri. Grandmother Young watched the performance and thought it very funny that a two-year-old could slap his knees and laugh so loudly at a jumping frog.

Then I remember another incident at the same farm when my mother dropped me from an upstairs window into the arms of my Uncle Harrison Young, who had come to see the new baby, my brother Vivian.

I was named for ... Harrison Young. I was given the diminutive Harry and, so that I could have two initials in my given name, the letter S was added. My Grandfather Truman's name was Anderson Shippe Truman and my Grandfather Young's name was Solomon Young, so I received the S for both of them. . . .

We moved from the Cass County farm to the old home of my mother's father in Jackson County. Grandfather Truman lived with us and he made a favorite out of me, as did my Grandfather Young. . . .

My brother Vivian was two years my junior and he had lovely long curls. Grandpa and I cut off his curls one day by putting him in a highchair out on the south porch. Mamma was angry enough to spank us both, but she had such respect for her father that she only frowned at him. One day after the hair-cutting episode I sat on the edge of a chair in front of the mirror to comb my hair—I fell off the chair backwards and broke my collarbone—my first but not my last broken bone. Later in this same room I was eating a peach and swallowed the seed. Almost choked to death but mamma pushed the seed down my throat with her finger and I lived to tell about it.

~1889~

When I was five and Vivian was three we were presented with a sister—Mary Jane, named for her Grandmother Truman. We heard her cry upstairs and thought we had a new pet until our father told us we had a new sister. . . .

My father bought me a Shetland pony about this time, and a beautiful little saddle—my brother's granddaughter has the saddle now. I'd ride with my father on my little Shetland and he on his big horse. He'd lead my pony and I felt perfectly safe—but one day coming down the north road toward the house I fell off the pony and had to walk about half a mile to the house. My father said that a boy who was not able to stay on a pony at a walk ought to walk himself. Mamma thought I was badly mistreated but I wasn't, in spite of my crying all the way to the house. I learned a lesson.

~1890~

The Truman family moves to Independence, Missouri.

When I was six, Vivian three, and Mary one year old, we moved to Independence. Mamma was anxious we should have town schooling. About this time my eyes became a problem and mamma took me to Dr. Thompson in Kansas City. . . . Glasses were fitted by Dr. Thompson and I've worn practically the same prescription ever since.

~1892–1895~

Harry Truman enters the first grade at Noland School.

When I was eight I started to school at the Noland School on South Liberty Street. My first grade teacher was Miss Myra Ewing, a grand woman. That first year in school made a profound impression on me. I learned to get along with my classmates and also learned a lot from Appleton's *First Reader*, learned how to add and subtract, and stood in well with my teacher.

In my second school year Miss Minnie Ward was my teacher. She was a good teacher and a lovely woman. . . .

Along in January my brother and I had a terrible case of diphtheria—no antitoxin in those days. They gave us ipecac and whiskey. I've hated the smell of both since. . . .

I was paralyzed for six months after the throat disease left me, and my mother wheeled me around in a baby buggy. My arms, legs and throat were of no use, but I recovered and went back to school and skipped the third grade.

~1896–1901~

In 1896 we moved to a nice house at Waldo Avenue and River Boulevard. . . . The grand times we had! Halloween parties and all sorts of meetings after school, making bridges by Caesar's plans and discussing what we'd like to be when grown up. We published a high school paper in 1901, called *The Gleam* for Tennyson's "Follow the Gleam." It is still published by the Independence High School after fifty years.

~1901~

When I graduated from high school in May, 1901, it was expected by the family and by me that there would be some chance for more education. Difficulties overtook us which resulted in the loss of the family farm of 160 acres and of the home place at Waldo and River Boulevard in Independence. It was necessary that some addition be made to the family income. So I got a job as timekeeper on a railroad construction outfit under L. J. Smith. . . . My salary was thirty-five dollars a month and board. . . . I was furnished with a tricycle car. Its power was by hand and I furnished the power.

~1902–1903~

On August 10, 1902, Harry Truman starts employment in the mailroom of the *Kansas City Star* at $7 a week. In October he goes to work for the National Bank of Commerce.

After working some eight or ten months for the railroad contractor, the job ended by being completed and I went to work for the Kansas City *Star* "wrapping singles" in the mailing department at nine dollars a week—a raise in pay. Then one of my friends came along early in 1903 or late in 1902 and I went to work in the basement of the National Bank of Commerce at Tenth and Walnut, Kansas City, Missouri, as a clerk at thirty-five dollars a month. At that time we lived at 2108 Park Avenue in Kansas City.

My brother and I worked at the bank and my father worked at an elevator in the east bottoms. In 1904, my father traded the house at 2108 Park for an equity in 80 acres in Henry County, Missouri, and late in 1904 the family moved to Clinton.

I went to board at 1314 Troost Avenue with some of the bank boys.

~1905~

Early in 1905 I quit the National Bank of Commerce and went to work for the Union National Bank. . . . I wasn't long at the Union National Bank until I was getting $100 a month—a magnificent salary in Kansas City in 1905.

~1909–1911~

On February 9, 1909, Truman receives his first degree in the Masonic Order, Belton Lodge No. 450 at Belton, Missouri. In 1910 he is elected junior warden of his lodge. In 1911 he organizes a lodge at Grandview and is made master Upper Division.

~1914–1915~

Harry Truman is named road overseer of Washington Township, Missouri, a post that had been held by his late father.

When my father passed away in 1914 I was appointed road overseer in his place and served until the presiding judge became dissatisfied because I gave the county too much for the money. In the meantime Congressman Borland appointed me postmaster at Grandview. I let a widow woman who was helping to raise and educate her younger sisters and brothers run the office as assistant postmaster and take the pay which amounted to about fifty dollars a month—a lot of money in those days. It would have paid two farmhands.

Along in 1915 I met a promoter by the name of Jerry Culbertson, through one of our farmer neighbors. Mr. Culbertson interested Mr. [Thomas] Hughes [a farmer friend] and me in a zinc and lead mine at Commerce, Oklahoma, and I undertook to run it, along with a red-haired hoisting engineer by the name of Bill Throop. Bill was all wool and a yard wide but we couldn't make our mine pay. He asked me to raise $2,500 and buy a drilling machine and go up north of Pitcher, Oklahoma and prospect the land up there for lead and zinc. But I'd already put all my ready money into the Commerce mine and couldn't raise the $2,500. If I'd done it we'd both be rolling in wealth today. The Commerce mine petered out and I lost $2,000.

I got all patriotic and joined the army. My partners got into a fuss and let that lease go to pot. Another company took it over and drilled a well on it and there was never a dry hole found on that 320 acres. It was the famous Teter Pool. If I'd stayed home and run my oil company I'd have been a millionaire. But I always did let ethics beat me out of money and I suppose I always will.

~1916–1917~

Truman invests $5,000 in the Atlas-Okla Oil Lands Syndicate and becomes treasurer of the new company on September 25, 1916. The firm goes out of business in 1917 when the U.S. enters World War I.

~1917–1919~

Truman serves in World War I as a captain in the 129th Field Artillery of the Thirty-Fifth Division.

I was stirred in heart and soul by the war messages of Woodrow Wilson, and since I'd joined the National Guard at twenty-one I thought I ought to go. I believe that the great majority of the country were stirred by the same flame that stirred me in those great days. I felt that I was a Galahad after the Grail and I'll never forget how my love cried on my shoulder when I told her I was going. That was worth a lifetime on this earth.

When President Wilson declared war on April 6, 1917, however, I helped to expand Batteries B and C into a regiment. At the organization of Battery F, I was elected a first lieutenant. I had not expected to be more than a second lieutenant and would have been happy just to remain a sergeant. I made arrangements for my sister and a good man we had on the farm to take over its operation and I set to work to be a field artillery man sure enough.

On September 26, 1917, we arrived at Camp Doniphan located just west of and adjoining Fort Sill, Oklahoma. My duties really piled up after we arrived at camp. Not only was it expected of me to do regular duty as a first lieutenant in Battery F but the colonel made me regimental canteen officer.

~1918~

After receiving a high commendation, Harry writes proudly home to Bess about it, and adds as an afterthought, "I suppose you will have to spend the rest of your life taking the conceit out of me."

My mother and sister came to see me at Camp Doniphan. My mother was sixty-five years old but she never shed a tear, smiled at me all the time and told me to do my best for my country. But she cried all the way home. . . .

I was ordered overseas with the special school detail of the division. We left Doniphan on March 20 about noon by the Rock Island and arrived at Kansas City at 4:00 A.M. I got a switchman out in the Rosedale yards to let me use his phone and I called my mother and my sweetheart. It was the last time I talked to either for a year and two months.

On March 30, the day before Easter Sunday, we sailed aboard the *George Washington* for France. There we were watching New York's skyline diminish and wondering if we'd be heroes or corpses. Most of us got by without being either....

On the tenth of July the colonel (Dick Burleson) sent for me. I went over everything I'd done for the last ten days to see if I could find out what I was to be bawled out for, but could think of nothing. I waited around in his office until he'd dressed down a second lieutenant or two and then my time came. He suddenly said to me, "Harry, how would you like to command a battery?"

"Well, sir," I said, "I hope to be able to do that some day."

"All right, you'll take command of D Battery in the morning."

I saluted, about-faced and walked out. Then I told the major that my tour of duty in France would be short because Klemm had given me D Battery. They were the wild Irish and German Catholics from Rockhurst Academy in Kansas City. They had had four commanders before me. I wasn't a Catholic, I was a thirty-second degree Mason. I could just see my hide on the fence when I tried to run that outfit.

I've been very badly frightened several times in my life and the morning of July 11, 1918, when I took over that battery was one of those times. I was most anxious to make good in my new rank of captain and I was rather doubtful of my ability to handle that obstreperous battery. For some reason or other we hit it off . . .

Captain Truman went to the front on August 18, 1918.

I fired 3,000 rounds of 75 ammunition from 4:00 A.M. to 8:00 A.M., September 26, 1918. I had slept in the edge of a wood to the right of my battery position on Friday night. If

I hadn't awaked and got up at 4:00 A.M. I would not be here, because the Germans fired a barrage on my sleeping place!

At eight o'clock my battery pulled out for the front. As we marched on a road under an embankment, a French 155-mm. battery fired over my head and I still have trouble hearing what goes on when there is a noise. I went back and told the French captain what I thought of him but he couldn't understand me—so it made no difference.

We came to the front line at a little town, what was left of it, called Boureuilles.

Finally went into position on a road between Varennes and Cheppy about 10:00 P.M., September 28. In going into position I rode my horse under a tree and a limb of the tree scraped my glasses off—and I picked them up from the horse's back behind the saddle! No one would believe a tale like that but it happened.

I put the battery into position and then moved into an orchard a half mile ahead the next day. Fired on three batteries, destroyed one and put the other two out of business. The regimental colonel threatened me with a court martial for firing out of the Thirty-fifth Division sector! But I saved some men in the Twenty-eighth Division on our left and they were grateful in 1948!

On April 17, 1918, Captain Truman writes home to reassure his fiancée: "Have only seen one good-looking French woman and she was married to some French general or admiral or something, anyway he had seven or eight yards of gold braid on him."

They went to the front August 18, 1918, and stayed there until November 11, 1918, under my command and were brought home and discharged May 6, 1919 and all their discharges were signed by me. They took up a collection and bought me a big silver cup with a most beautiful inscription on it and they all continue to call me Captain Harry.

After my discharge I went back to the farm and on June 28, 1919, my wedding to Miss Bess Wallace took place— the same beautiful, blue-eyed, gold haired girl referred to earlier in this manuscript.

Harry Truman marries his childhood sweetheart Bess (Elizabeth Virginia) Wallace and settles down on the family farm, facing heavy debts.

When my grandmother died there was a will contest and a settlement which placed a back-breaking mortgage of about $30,000 on the farm.

Very bad years, both wet and dry, added to the difficulty so that interest and overhead kept the debt right around $35,000.

My canteen sergeant being a furnishing goods man wanted to open a store on Twelfth Street in Kansas City so I established a line of credit with a couple of banks and we opened a men's furnishing store at 104 West Twelfth along late in 1919. A flourishing business was carried on for about a year and a half and then came the squeeze of 1921.

Jacobson and I went to bed one night with a $35,000 inventory and awoke the next day with a $25,000 shrink-age. . . . This brought bills payable and bank notes due at such a rapid rate we went out of business.

All the bank notes were paid off and the merchandise bills were settled as equitably as could be managed. It took several years to clean everything up. The store was finally closed in the latter part of 1922.

The haberdashery fails during the depression of 1920–21. Refusing to go into bankruptcy, Harry Truman pays off debts totaling around $12,000 in full over the next fifteen years.

~1922–1923~

Truman runs for his first elective office and is elected eastern district judge of the Jackson County Court.

> Early in March, 1922, the Democrats began talking about candidates for county judge for the eastern district of Jackson County.
>
> Well, the store was closing up—I liked the political game and I knew personally half the people in eastern Jackson County. I also had kinfolks in nearly every precinct and I decided to make the race. It was a hot affair. I opened my campaign in Lee's Summit with Colonel (now Major General) E. M. Strayton making the principal address. . . . He knew my war record, what there was of it, and he made the most of it. From June 1 to August 5, 1922, I made every township and precinct in the county and when the votes were counted on the first Tuesday in August, I had a plurality of 500 votes.
>
> The election in the fall went off without incident because eastern Jackson is as Democratic as Mississippi or South Carolina. I was sworn in on January 1, 1923.

Truman enrolls in Kansas City Law School on October 5, 1923.

~1924–1925~

A daughter, Mary Margaret Truman, is born on February 17, 1924, in Kansas City.

Truman is appointed district deputy grand master in the 59th Masonic District.

On November 6, Truman loses his bid for reelection as county commissioner by 877 votes (the only election defeat of his career).

He is forty-one years old, jobless, "completely broke and without much prospect of being any other way."

During 1925 and the early part of 1926 I put on a whirl-wind membership campaign for the Kansas City Automobile Club and made a good living at it.

Truman receives good grades but withdraws from Kansas City Law School in the second year.

~1926–1929~

Truman runs for office again in 1926. On November 2 he is elected presiding judge of the Jackson County Court, a post he will hold until 1934.

There was no opposition in the primary and my majority in the fall election was a little over 16,000 votes.

I set to work as presiding judge to clean up the county's financial condition.

~1930~

Harry Truman is reelected as presiding judge by a healthy margin.

It is generally conceded that Jackson County, Missouri, came out with a good road system and a good set of public buildings. When the election of 1930 came up we were in the midst of the building and budget reform programs so the presiding judge and associate judges favorable to the policy being pursued were returned to office. The majority of the presiding judge was over 58,000 votes. It was in fact a vote of confidence.

~1932–1934~

I helped arrange the Fourth District because my ambition was to become a member of the House of Representatives. I believed I could go to the House from the new Fourth District and stay as long as I chose to stay but when the party caucus was held to decide on candidates in the 1934 election from Jackson my good friend Judge C. Jasper Bell had talked T. J. Pendergast into endorsing him for congressman from the Fourth District and my plan to be a congressman went out the window. I decided to go back to the farm and stay out of politics but that didn't help either.

~1934~

At age fifty Harry Truman decides to run for the U.S. Senate.

Along in the first week in May I was speaking in Warsaw, Missouri, on the bond issue when I received a phone call from Sedalia, which is about thirty miles from Warsaw, asking me to stop at the Bothwell Hotel on my way north and have a talk with James P. Aylward, the state chairman of the Democratic Committee and Jim Pendergast, nephew of T.J. and my war buddy.

I stopped and talked to them and they urged me to run for the nomination to the United States Senate. I told them that I had no legislative experience, that I thought I was something of an executive and I'd rather wait two years and run for governor. But they insisted that I owed it to the party to run. . . .

It was a tough three-cornered race. When the smoke blew away, I was nominated by some 40,000 plurality. . . . I carried forty counties outside Jackson and ran second in sixty. My wide acquaintance in the state and particularly my association with county judges and county clerks is the answer to my being able to win with the support of the Kansas City organization, while Charles M. Howell, . . . widely known lawyer and insurance man, could not. I made a very strenuous campaign, covering practically the whole state outside St. Louis, and I think showed that people would vote for me.

On August 7, 1934, Truman wins the Democratic primary for the Senate seat.

On November 6 Harry Truman is elected Senator.

> The election in the fall of 1934 was a pushover for the Democrats so I came to the United States Senate and went to work. I was in luck on committee assignments: Interstate Commerce, Appropriations, and a couple of minor ones—Printing, and Public Buildings and Grounds.

~1935–1940~

Harry Truman is sworn in as a senator by Vice-President John Nance Garner on January 3, 1935.

Senator Truman becomes known as a "patient and persistent" member of the subcommittee of the Interstate Commerce Committee on railroad finance.

> The work of that subcommittee finally resulted in the Wheeler-Truman Bill—the Transportation Act of 1940. . . . And after two years of hard work on it and three years of hearings on railroad finance methods, it became law.
>
> I learned much about procedure in the Senate, about New York banker and lawyer methods and how the House and Senate came to conclusions on legislation during this time. . . .
>
> During my first term as senator I was chairman of the subcommittee of the Interstate Commerce Committee out of which came the Civil Aeronautics Act. Senator Donahey of Ohio was appointed chairman of that subcommittee but did not attend the meetings. Senator Austin of Vermont and I carried on the hearings over a couple of years and finally presented a bill to the Senate which became the Civil Aeronautics Act.

~1940~

Truman becomes Grand Master of Missouri, the highest-ranking freemason in the state.

It looked very dark for the junior senator from Missouri but he stayed by his friends and when the smoke cleared away and the votes were counted he was still the junior senator from Missouri. People like public servants who serve them and they like friendship and loyalty to friends. Friends don't count in fair weather. It is when trouble comes that friends count.

I was nominated by a plurality of 8,400 votes in the August primary, after the most bitter, mud-slinging campaign in Missouri's history of dirty campaigns. At eleven o'clock on the night of the primary vote I went to bed eleven thousand votes behind and supposedly defeated. The Kansas City *Star* and the St. Louis *Post-Dispatch* had extras out telling how happy they were and safe Missouri was from my slimy person as senator.

A lying press cannot fool the people. I came back to the Senate and the double-crossing ingrate of a governor was sent back to the nursery.

Harry Truman wins reelection to the U.S. Senate on November 5.

~1941~

I started my second term as junior senator from Missouri on January 3, 1941. After the election and in between I'd been working on military and naval appropriations. . . . Our situation was shocking. *We had no defenses.* In 1940 was passed a Universal Service Law. . . . I had been training reserve officers at camps and in night schools from 1920 to 1940, so I went down to see Chief of Staff, General Marshall, and told him I'd like to quit the Senate and go into service as a field artillery colonel and an instructor in F.A. tactics.

He asked how old I was and I told him I was fifty-six years old. He pulled his reading glasses down on his nose, grinned at me and said, "We don't need old stiffs like you—this will be a young man's war."

He was right, of course, but it hurt my feelings and I decided to do something for the war effort on a constructive basis. After we had appropriated about twenty-five billions of dollars for national defense I took my old coupe and began inspecting camp construction and naval installations from Maine to Florida and from Pennsylvania to New Mexico, California, Washington and along both borders north and south. Some 30,000 miles were covered. This while the bitter Missouri election campaign was on also.

On February 18, 1941, I made a statement to the Senate on what I'd seen, and asked that a special committee be authorized to look into defense expenditures. I believe that statement resulted in the savings of billions of the taxpayers' money and thousands of lives of our fighting men.

~1941–1944~

Truman wins national recognition as chairman of the Special Committee to Investigate the National Defense Program.

~1944~

On July 27, 1944, Harry Truman is nominated as vice-president to run with President Roosevelt in FDR's quest for a fourth term.

When the 1944 election was approaching mention began to be made about Truman for vice president. Every effort was made by me to shut it off. I liked my job as a senator and I wanted to stay with it. It takes a long time for a man to establish himself in the Senate. I was a member of three very important standing committees—Appropriations, Interstate Commerce, and Military Affairs—and was well up on the list on all of them for seniority, which is very important. My Special Commitee was doing good work and I wanted to stay with it.

I had tried to make it very plain wherever I went that I was not a candidate for vice president. While it is a very high office and one of honor, I did not want it. I liked my job as senator from Missouri, and since I couldn't get into the armed forces, as I wanted to, I felt I was making a contribution to the war effort as chairman of the Special Committee and as member of the Military Affairs Committee and the Military Subcommittee on Appropriations. . . .

On Thursday before the vice president was to be nominated [Democratic party leader Bob] Hannegan called me and asked me to come over to the Blackstone Hotel to a meeting of the Democratic leaders. I went. . . .

They began to put pressure on me to allow my name to be presented to the convention. I said no and kept saying it. Hannegan had put in a call to San Diego for the president. When the connection was made I sat on one twin bed and Bob on the other. When the president used the phone he always talked in such a strong voice it was necessary to hold the phone away from your ear to keep from being deafened. I could hear both ends of the conversation.

Finally Roosevelt said, "Bob, have you got that fellow lined up yet?"

Bob said, "No, he is the contrariest Missouri mule I've ever dealt with."

The president then said, "Well, you tell him if he wants to break up the Democratic Party in the middle of a war that's his responsibility" and bang up went the phone.

To say I was stunned is to put it mildly. I sat for a minute or two and then began walking around the room. All the people in the room were watching me and not saying a word.

Finally I said, "Well, if that is the situation I'll have to say yes, but why the hell didn't he tell me in the first place."

I learned that President Roosevelt had called a meeting at the White House of the political leaders in the party to discuss the situation with regard to the nomination of a vice president at the coming Democratic convention. . . .

Wallace, Douglas, Jim Byrnes and Truman were discussed. After some acrimonious debate the president told them he thought Truman would be the best candidate. He gave Hannegan a note in longhand which said, "Bob, Truman is the man. F.D.R."

Harry Truman accepts the vice-presidential nomination at a late hour with the shortest speech of the convention: "I don't know what else I can say, except that I accept this great honor with all humility. I thank you." The speech is received by the weary delegates with an ovation.

After the nomination and my return to the hotel with police and secret service none of us was happy. But we all faced the situation and have been facing it ever since.

The next day we boarded a Southern Pacific train and began a cross-country tour. Beaumont, Houston, San Antonio, Uvalde where I had a grand visit with Mr. Garner, El Paso, Tucson, and finally Los Angeles.

* Then to San Francisco, Portland, Seattle and across the northern part of the country on the Chicago, Milwaukee and Pacific railroad.

Stopped at all the towns of any consequence, told the newspaper at Spokane what a lousy sheet it is, addressed a labor conference and then went on east. That trip was the first "whistle stop" campaign . . .

On November 7, Roosevelt and Truman win the election, defeating the Republican ticket of Thomas E. Dewey and John W. Bricker by more than 3.5 million votes.

~1945~

On January 20 Harry Truman is inaugurated as Vice-President.

On April 12 President Roosevelt dies of a stroke in Warm Springs, Georgia.

About five o'clock on the afternoon of that fateful April 12, 1945, the senate recessed and I walked over to the office of the speaker of the house, Mr. Rayburn.

I was informed as soon as I arrived that Mr. Early, the press secretary of the president, wanted me to call the White House. As soon as I could talk to Mr. Early, he told me to come to the White House as quickly as possible, to come in by way of the Pennsylvania Avenue entrance, and to come to Mrs. Roosevelt's study.

When I arrived I was informed that the president had passed away. It was a real shock when Mrs. Roosevelt made the announcement to me. The secretary of state came in immediately and after offering to do anything I could for Mrs. Roosevelt, I told Mr. Stettinius to call a cabinet meeting.

I was sworn in as president at 7:09 P.M. ... on the evening of April 12, 1945, as Chief Justice Harlan Fiske Stone swore me in as president of the United States in the Cabinet Room at the White House, underneath a portrait of Woodrow Wilson. And as I've already admitted, I was plenty scared. But scared or not, and prepared or not, I promised myself one thing that evening, and in the days and nights that followed: that I'd work damn hard and try damn hard to be a good President.

After attending the president's funeral, I went to Congress with a message.

On May 7, Germany surrendered. The announcement was made on May 8, my sixty-first birthday.

May 8, 1945

Dear Mama & Mary,

I am sixty-one this morning, and I slept in the President's room in the White House last night. They have finished the painting and have some of the furniture in place. I'm hoping it will be ready for you by Friday.

This will be a historical day. At 9:00 this morning I must make a broadcast to the country: announcing the German surrender. The papers were signed yesterday morning and hostilities will cease on all fronts at midnight tonight. Isn't that some birthday present?

Harry

On July 2, 1945, President Truman addresses the Senate to urge ratification of the United Nations charter, saying, "It comes from the reality of experience in a world where one generation has failed twice to keep the peace."

Mr. Churchill called me . . . and wanted a meeting with me and Prime Minister Stalin of Russia. Later on a meeting was agreed upon and Stalin, Churchill and I met at Potsdam to implement the agreements made at Tehran and Yalta.

On July 22, during the Potsdam conference, Truman and Churchill decide to drop the atomic bomb if Japan does not accept the Potsdam Proclamation calling for unconditional surrender.

At the time, the Potsdam meeting was considered a success. Russia agreed to enter the Japanese war, the use of the atomic bomb was decided. We came away from the meeting feeling that we were well on the road to world peace.

The bomb was dropped on Japan and Japan surrendered.

On August 6 and August 9 atomic bombs are dropped on Hiroshima and Nagasaki.

On August 14 President Truman announces the Japanese surrender.

On September 6 Truman sends his Twenty-one Point Address to Congress, containing most of his domestic program (later called the Fair Deal).

After his Christmas vacation is cut short in December, Truman writes a letter home to his wife:

December 28, 1945

Dear Bess:

Well I'm here in the White House, the great white sepulcher of ambitions and reputations. I feel like a last year's bird's nest which is on its second year. Not very often I admit I am not in shape. I think maybe that exasperates you too, as a lot of other things I do and pretend to do exasperate you. But it isn't intended for that purpose. . . .

You can never appreciate what it means to come home as I did the other evening after doing at least 100 things I didn't want to do and have the only person in the world whose approval and good opinion I value, look at me like I'm something the cat dragged in and tell me I've come in at last because I couldn't find any reason to stay away.

I wonder why we are made so that what we really think and feel we cover up?

This head of mine should have been bigger and better proportioned. There ought to have been more brain and a larger bump of ego or something to give me an idea that there can be a No. 1 man in the world. I didn't want to be. But, in spite of opinion to the contrary, *Life* & *Time* say I am.

If that is the case, Margie and everyone else who may have any influence on my actions must give me help and assistance. . . . If I can get the use of the best brains in the country and a little bit of help from those I have on a pedestal at home the job will be done. . . .

Kiss my baby and I love you in season & out.

Harry

~1946~

Truman signs the Employment Act of 1946 on February 20.

On May 25 Truman asks for legislation to draft striking workers into the army under certain conditions.

On August 1 Truman signs the Atomic Energy Act of 1946.

~1947~

On March 12 Truman delivers the "Truman Doctrine" speech, asking for $400 million to defend Greece and Turkey against the danger of Communist control. "I believe that it must be the policy of the United States," he tells Congress, "to support free peoples who are resisting attempted subjugation by armed minorities or outside pressures."

On July 26 President Truman signs the National Security Act of 1947, unifying the armed forces.

In 1947 my mother lay for weeks on a rocking bed suffering no end. When she finally passed on I was over in Cincinnati and instinctively I knew she'd gone. I'd been dozing and dreamed she'd said "Goodbye, Harry. Be a good boy." When Dr. Graham came in to my room on the Sacred Cow I knew what he would say.

On October 29 Truman receives the report of the President's Commission on Civil Rights, *To Secure These Rights*.

~1948~

On February 2 President Truman submits his ten-point civil rights program to Congress, calling for reforms including a federal law against lynching and an end to segregation in the military.

On April 3 President Truman signs the Foreign Assistance Act (providing $12.4 billion to Europe over four years), implementing the Marshall Plan.

On May 14 the U.S. recognizes the new state of Israel.

On June 24 Truman orders an airlift to counter the Soviet blockade of Berlin.

On July 26 Truman issues Executive Order 9981 to end racial segregation in the armed services.

Although Thomas Dewey leads in the polls, Harry Truman wins the election on November 2, scoring the most sensational upset in U.S. political history—polling 24,105,695 votes to Dewey's 21,969,170.

~1949~

On January 5, in a State of the Union message, President Truman outlines the Fair Deal program, calling for extension and expansion of FDR's New Deal ("Every segment of our population and every individual has the right to expect from our government a fair deal.").

On January 20 President Truman delivers his Inaugural Address, containing a stirring defense of democracy.

Truman signs the North Atlantic Treaty on April 4 and the Housing Act of 1949, his major reform achievement, on July 15.

On September 23 Truman announces that an atomic bomb has been detected in the Soviet Union.

On October 6 Truman signs the Mutual Defense Assistance Act, providing aid to North Atlantic Treaty members.

~1950~

On January 31 President Truman announces an order to construct a hydrogen bomb.

On June 24 the President learns of a North Korean attack on South Korea and on June 30 commits ground troops to the support of South Korea.

On June 28 President Truman appoints General Douglas A. MacArthur head of the American forces in Korea.

On October 14 President Truman confers with General MacArthur on Wake Island.

An assassination attempt on November 1 by two Puerto Rican nationalist gunmen leaves President Truman unharmed but not unaffected.

> Because two crackpots or crazy men tried to shoot me a few days ago my good and efficient guards are nervous. So I'm trying to be as helpful as I can. Would very much like to take a walk this morning but the S.S. say that there are more crackpots around and the "Boss" and Margie are worried about me—so I won't take my usual walk. It's hell to be President of the Greatest Most Powerful Nation on Earth—I'd rather be "first in the Iberian Village."

~1951~

On April 11 President Truman relieves General Douglas MacArthur of command because of insubordination and unwillingness to see the war limited to Korea.

On July 10 Korean cease-fire talks open after U.N. forces repulse the North Korean advance into South Korea.

President Truman delivers his "Real Americanism" speech on August 15, speaking out against McCarthyism and "character assassination."

~1952~

On March 29, President Truman, now 67 years old, announces he will not run for reelection.

On April 8, to prevent a scheduled strike, Truman issues an order seizing steel mills. The mills' seizure is struck down by the Supreme Court on June 2.

On November 4 Dwight D. Eisenhower and his running mate, Richard M. Nixon, are elected in a landslide.

Diary, November 24, 1952
5 A.M.

The White House is as quiet as a church. I can hear the planes at the airport warming up. As always there is a traffic roar—sounds like wind and rain through the magnolias.

Bess' mother is dying across the hallway. She was 90 years old August 4th. Vivian's mother-in-law passed on Saturday at eleven thirty. She was also ninety just a month after or before Mrs. Wallace. When you are sixty-eight death watches come often.

~1953~

Truman attends the inauguration of President Eisenhower on January 20 and returns with Bess to Independence, where he can take his morning walks without being followed by reporters.

This morning at 7 A.M. I took off for my morning walk . . .

I went on down Van Horn Road (some call it Truman Road now) and took a look at the work progressing on the widening for a two way traffic line through the county seat . . . The boss or the contractor was looking on and I asked him if he didn't need a good strawboss. He took a look at me and then watched the work a while and then took another look and broke out in a broad smile and said "Oh yes! You *are* out of a job aren't you."

—diary, Independence, Missouri, May 20, 1953

~1954~

At age seventy Harry Truman records in his diary that he is still walking two miles "most every morning." He spends much of his time writing his *Memoirs* and delivers a 500,000-word manuscript on July 4.

~1955–1956~

The *Memoirs* are published in two volumes, *Year of Decisions* (1955) and *Years of Trial and Hope* (1956).

> I guess I'll have to state the few interesting facts of my life without the introspective trimmings with which most so-called writers and half-baked essayists clutter up the printed page.

—post-presidential files, memoirs, January 16, 1954

~1956~

On April 21, 1956, Harry Truman attends the wedding of his daughter Margaret to Clifton Daniel of the *New York Times*.

Harry and Bess Truman leave on May 8, his 72nd birthday, for a seven-week trip, touring Europe by train.

On June 20 Truman receives an honorary degree from Oxford.

~1957~

In July Truman attends the dedication of the Truman Library.

~1958~

On February 19 Truman accepts a position as Chubb Fellow at Yale.

~1959~

On April 13 Truman begins a series of lectures on the presidency at Columbia University.

~1960~

Truman completes a collection of essays, published in book form as *Mr. Citizen*, and campaigns for John F. Kennedy in the fall.

~1963~

As you know, I am just as interested in what goes on now as I was when I was in the center of things but that old lady "Anno Domini" has been chasing me and I have to slow up a little bit, particularly since she has a partner in Mrs. Truman.

—letter to Dean Acheson, May 14, 1963

~1964~

On his eightieth birthday Truman tells reporters: "Remember me as I was, not as I am."

On May 9 Truman addresses the Senate, becoming the first former president to exercise "the privilege of the floor" and address the Senate in formal session.

~1966~

On January 21 President Lyndon Johnson presents Harry Truman with Medicare Card #1 in recognition of the fact that Truman was the first president to propose a system similar to Medicare. Truman responds, "You have made me very happy."

~1971~

On May 6 Truman refuses to accept the Congressional Medal of Honor, writing: "I do not consider that I have done anything which should be the reason for any award, congressional or otherwise."

~1972~

On December 5 Harry Truman is hospitalized for lung congestion.

On December 26 at 7:50 A.M., eighty-eight-year-old Harry Truman dies in Kansas City's Research Hospital and Medical Center.

At his own request he is buried in the courtyard of the Harry S. Truman Library ("so I can get up and walk into my office if I want to").

ADDITIONAL REFERENCES

INTRODUCTION: *Trumanisms:* Truman, Margaret, 1973, 29, 118, 457, 595, 634; McCullough, 155, 558, 861, 897; Miller, 16, 26; ACORN THINKING: speech, Missoula, Montana, May 12, 1950; ADAMS, JOHN: Truman, Margaret, 1989, 244; ADAMS, JOHN QUINCY: Truman, Margaret, 1989, 266; ADVANTAGES: Truman, 1964; AD-VICE: Truman, Margaret, 1973, 367; Simpson, 1957, 167; Truman 1960a, 202; Truman, 1960b, 113; *New York Times*, September 20, 1964; AFFABILITY: Truman, Margaret, 1973, 175; AMERICANS: Ferrell, 1980b, 44; ATOM: Truman, 1956, 315; ATOMIC AGE: Ferrell, 1980a, 121; ATOMIC BOMB: Truman, Margaret, 1973, 298; Truman, 1955, 417, 419–20; BARUCH, BERNARD: Ferrell, 1980b, 87; BILLIONS: press conference, January 8, 1947; BIPARTI-SAN: Settel, 37; BORED: Miller, 49; BOSSES: Truman, Margaret, 1973, 25; Columbia University, April 28, 1959; BRITISH: Kirkendall, 33; BROTHERHOOD: Daniels, 339; BUSINESSMAN: Settel, 38; CAPITAL PUNISHMENT:

Truman, 1960b, 119; CASTRO, FIDEL: Miller, 349; CATS: press conference, February 1, 1947; CHILDREN: Ferrell, 1994, 451; CHRISTMAS: Settel, 44; CHURCH: Poen, 1982, 29; Truman, Margaret, 1973, 74; memorandum for Tony Vaccaro, April 12, 1950; CHURCHILL, WINSTON: Acheson, 595; Poen, 1984, 195; Truman, 1955, 363; CLEVELAND, GROVER: Truman, Margaret, 1989, 13; COLD: Truman, Margaret, 1973, 24; COLLEGE: Steinberg, 427; COMMUNICATION: Truman, 1960a, 277; COMMUNISM: Public Papers, 1948, 289; CONGRESS: Settel, 51; CONSULTANT: Truman, Margaret, 1973, 603; COOLIDGE, CALVIN: Truman, Margaret, 1989, 45; Truman, 1956, 203; Letter to Hugh Ellis, December 6, 1954; COURAGE: McCullough, 60; CRACKPOTS: Truman, 1956, 271; CRAPS: Truman, Margaret, 1973, 83; CREDIT: Grand Forks, North Dakota, September 29, 1952; CUSTER, GENERAL GEORGE: Truman, Margaret, 1989, 284; DECISION-MAKING: Truman, 1960a, 265; Ferrell, 1980a, 116–17; DE GAULLE, CHARLES: Poen, 1984, 197; DEMOCRACY: Hillman, 13; DEMOCRATIC PARTY: McCullough, 960; DIGNITARIES: Ferrell, 1980b, 138; DISNEYLAND: Truman, Margaret, 1973, 617; DREAM: Farewell address, Washington, D.C., January 15, 1953; ECONOMIST: quoted in *New York Times*, April 14, 1985; McCullough, 558; Boller, 288; EDUCATION: Public Papers, 1948, 328; Truman, 1956, 271; EGOTIST: Ferrell, 1980b, 323; EISENHOWER, DWIGHT: Ferrell, 1994, 449–50; Truman, Margaret, 1973, 585; Truman, Margaret, 1989, 62, 65, 68–69; Ferrell, 1980b, 26; Diary, August 19, 1952; ENGLAND: McCullough, 957; FAREWELL ADDRESS: Address, January 15, 1953; FATHER: McCullough, 941; FBI: Memorandum, May 12, 1945; FEELING: Washington, D.C., June 3, 1948; FINE PRINT: Hillman, 159; FLYING SAUCERS: press conference, July 10, 1947; Public Papers, 1947, 331; FOREIGN POLICY: Truman, 1956, 290; FRIEND: Ferrell, 1980a, 74; FULBRIGHT, WILLIAM: Steinberg, 405; FUTURE: Speech,

Pemberton, 8; JOHNSON, ANDREW: Truman, 1960b, 77; *The Quotable Truman*, 1994, 124; KENNEDY, JOHN F.: Letter to J. Neely Peacock, Jr., September 5, 1963; Settel, 97; Aurthur, August 1971; LEADER: *The Quotable Truman*, 1994, 46; LEADERSHIP: *The Wit and Wisdom of Politics*, 1992, 123; LEWIS, JOHN L.: Memorandum of December 11, 1946; LINCOLN, ABRAHAM: *The Quotable Truman*, 1994, 120; Truman, Margaret, 1989, 322; MacARTHUR, DOUGLAS: Ferrell, 1980b, 324; Ferrell, 1980b, 47; Truman, Margaret, 1989, 283; MADISON, JAMES: Gallen, 96; MARSHALL, GENERAL GEORGE: Hillman, 150; Ferrell, 1980b, 109; MARSHALL PLAN: Miller, 19; MARSHALS: Truman, Margaret, 1973, 280–81; MATERIAL THINGS: Public Papers, 1950, 463; McCARTHY, JOSEPH: Truman, 1960b, 123; McKINLEYISM: Amalgamated Clothing Workers Convention, Atlantic City, May 13, 1954; MEXICO: Truman, Margaret, 1973, 407; MILITARY LEADERS: Gallen, 126–27; Truman, 1956, 444; Interview with Edward R. Murrow on the CBS television program *See It Now*, February 2, 1958; MILITARY WASTE: Steinberg, 142; MISSOURI WALTZ: Interview with Edward R. Murrow, February 2, 1958; MOLOTOV, VYACHESLAV: Ferrell, 1980b, 305; MONEY MAKING: McCullough, 99; MORNING: Hersey, 33–34; MUSIC: Hillman, 203; Pemberton, 6; NATION: Hillman, 232; NATIONAL HEALTH: Ferrell, 1980b, 165–66; NATIONAL HEALTH CARE: Truman, 1956, 17; NATIVE AMERICANS: Gallen, 60; Truman, 1960a, 175; Gallen, 60; Truman, Margaret, 1989, 282, 285; NEWS: Ferrell, 1980b, 194; NEWSPAPER PUBLISHERS: Williams, 20; NEWSPAPERS: McCullough, 155; NIXON, RICHARD: Steinberg, 425; Kirkendall, 257; Poen, 1982, 134; NUTS: Truman, Margaret, 1973, 361; OPPOSITION: Gallen, 83; ORATORS: Truman, 1989, 101; PAY-AS-YOU-GO: Hillman, 83; PEACE: Truman, 1956, x; Hillman, 86; Public Papers, 1948, 859; Public Papers, 1945, 405; Settel, 126, 174; PENDERGAST, T. J.: Letters and memoranda of

1949; PEOPLE: Truman, 1960a, 155; Donovan, 29; Hillman, 30; PESSIMISTS: Truman, 1960a, 97; Thompson, 9; PHYSICAL FITNESS: Hersey, 48; PIANO PLAYER: Hillman, 204; Aurthur, August 1971; PICASSO, PABLO: Ferrell, 1994, 398; PICTURES: Miller, 38; PIERCE, FRANKLIN: Truman, 1989, 11, 25; Truman, 1956, 196; PLAN: Public Papers, 1949, 546; President's Secretary's Files, Box 310; POETS: Vernon, 19; Miller, 429; POLITICIAN: Settel, 130; Truman, Margaret, 1973, 543; Hillman, 196; POLITICS: Ferrell, 1980a, 115–16; Public Papers, 1952–53, 220; Hillman, 198; Steinberg, 215; POLK, JAMES: Gallen, 108; POTSDAM: Letter to Dean Acheson, March 15, 1957 (unsent); Truman, Margaret, 1973, 275; POWER: Ferrell, 1980b, 177; PRESIDENCY: Barber, 271; Cunliffe, 326; Ferrell, 1980b, 176; PRESIDENTS: Truman, Margaret, 1973, 466; Truman, Margaret, 1989, 16, 20; Truman, 1956, 196; Truman, Margaret, 1973, 569; PRESIDENTS' RATINGS: Letter to Michael J. Kirwin, August 13, 1962; PRESS: Public Papers, 1948, 235; Truman, 1956, 414; Speech, Washington, D.C., February 23, 1958; Truman, Margaret, 1973, 24; Truman, Margaret, 1989, 50; Hersey, 43; Ferrell, 1980a, 116; PRESS CONFERENCE: Gallen, 47; PRIMA DONNAS: Truman, Margaret, 1973, 315; letter to "Mamma and Mary," September 22, 1945; PROBLEM-SOLVING: Donovan, 28; PROSPERITY: Hillman, 83; PUBLICITY HOUND: Williams, 140; PUBLIC SCHOOLS: Letter, December 5, 1962; PUBLIC SPEAKING: Truman, 1955, 161; READING: Letter to Martha Ann Truman Swoyer, November 4, 1971; Caldwell, 28; Robbins, 42; Ferrell, 1980a, 115; RECESSION: Frost, 70; RELIGION: Steinberg, 119; Gallen, 120; RELIGIOUS SECTS: Caldwell, 94; REPUBLICAN: Settel, 150; REPUBLICANS: Truman, 1964; Adler, 176; REPUBLICAN PARTY: Public Papers, 1948, 771; REWARD: PSF, "Longhand Notes, Harry S. Truman, County Judge," Box 334; Poen, 1984, 204; RIGHT: Kirkendall, 287; Williams, 183; Ferrell, 1980b, 127; ROGERS, WILL: Letter to Bess Truman, August 9,

1935; Poen, 1984, 98; ROOSEVELT, FRANKLIN D.: Gallen, 148, 149; Ferrell, 1994, 133; ROOSEVELT, THEODORE: Truman, 1956, 201; Truman, Margaret, 1989, 348; Gallen, 134; RUSSIANS: Truman, 1955, 70–71; Letter to Margaret Truman, March 3, 1948; Ferrell, 1994, 249; SENATE: Ferrell, 1980b, 201; SENATOR: McCullough, 213; Daniels, 177; Gridiron Club, Washington, D.C., May 11, 1947; SENIOR CITIZEN: Ferrell, 1980b, 408; SHORTEST SPEECH: Independence, Missouri, December 26, 1949; SLEEPING PILL: Truman, 1964; SMALL BUSINESS: Pemberton, 27; SNOBBERY: Truman, 1960a, 90; S.O.B.: National Press Club, Washington, D.C., May 10, 1954; SOCIALISM: Arkansas speech, July 2, 1952; STATESMAN: *New York World-Telegram & Sun*, April 12, 1958; STEVENSON, ADLAI: McCullough, 891; STUDENTS: *The Wit and Wisdom of the Twentieth Century*, 1987, 117; Letter to Martha Ann Truman Swoyer, November 4, 1971; TAFT, WILLIAM HOWARD: Truman, Margaret, 1989, 15; TAXES: Truman, 1956, 41; TAYLOR, ZACHARY: Truman, Margaret, 1989, 21; Truman, 1956, 195; TEACHER: Ferrell, 1980b, 167; Miller, 39; TELEVISION: Truman, 1960a, 153–54; THINK: Truman, 1960a, 97; TOP DOG: Daniels, 336; TRICKLE DOWN: Amalgamated Clothing Workers, Atlantic City, May 13, 1954; TRUMAN, BESS: Truman, Margaret, 1973, 59; TWAIN, MARK: Truman, Margaret, 1973, 335; TYLER, JOHN: Gallen, 107; ULCER PAY: Letters and memoranda of 1949; UNDERDOG: Truman, 1960b, 119; UNITED STATES: Hillman, 121; UNUSUAL PROCEDURE: Truman letters and memoranda of 1947; VAN BUREN, MARTIN: Truman, Margaret, 1989, 307; VICE-PRESIDENT: Truman, Margaret, 1989, 45, 372; WALKING: Truman, 1960a, 87–88; WAR: Donovan, 81; WAR PREVENTION: Truman, 1956, x, 383; Truman, 1955, 210; WARS: Public Papers, 1947, 187; WASHINGTON, D.C.: *New York Times*, March 10, 1989; Ferrell, 1980b, 72; WASHINGTON, GEORGE: Hillman, 13; Truman, Margaret, 1989, 103; Gallen, 79; WASHINGTON

BIBLIOGRAPHY

Acheson, Dean. *Present at the Creation: My Years in the State Department.* Hamish Hamilton, 1969.

Adler, Bill, ed. *Presidential Wit from Washington to Johnson.* Trident Press, 1966.

Aurthur, Robert Alan. "The Wit and Sass of Harry S. Truman." *Esquire,* August 1971.

Barber, James David. *The Presidential Character.* Prentice-Hall, 1972.

Bernstein, Barton, ed. *Politics and Policies of the Truman Administration.* Quadrangle Books, 1972.

Blair, Walter, & Hamlin Hill. *America's Humor: From Poor Richard to Doonesbury.* Oxford University Press, 1978.

Boller, Paul F. *Presidential Anecdotes.* Oxford University Press, 1981.

Caldwell, George S., ed. *Good Old Harry: The Wit and Wisdom of Harry S. Truman.* Hawthorn, 1966.

Cunliffe, Marcus. *American Presidents and the Presidency.* American Heritage Press, 1968.

Daniels, Jonathan. *The Man of Independence*. Lippincott, 1950.

Donovan, Robert. *The Words of Harry Truman*. Newmarker, 1984.

Ferrell, Robert H., ed. *The Autobiography of Harry S. Truman*. Colorado Associated University Press, 1980a.

———. *Off the Record: The Private Papers of Harry S. Truman*. Harper & Row, 1980b.

———. *Dear Bess: The Letters from Harry to Bess Truman*. Norton, 1983.

———. *Harry S. Truman: A Life*. University of Missouri Press, 1994.

Frost, Elizabeth. *The Bully Pulpit: Quotations from American Presidents*. Facts On File, 1988.

Gallen, David, ed. *The Quotable Truman*. Carroll & Graf, 1994.

Hedley, John Hollister. *Harry S. Truman: The "Little" Man from Missouri*. Barron's, 1979.

Henning, Chuck, ed. *The Wit and Wisdom of Politics*. Fulcrum, 1992.

Hersey, John. *Aspects of the Presidency*. Ticknor & Fields, 1980.

Hillman, William. *Mr. President*. Farrar, Straus and Young, 1952.

Jenkins, Roy. *Truman*. Harper & Row, 1986.

Kirkendall, Richard S., ed. *The Harry S. Truman Encyclopedia*. G. K. Hall, 1989.

McCullough, David. *Truman*. Simon & Schuster, 1992.

Mencken, H. L. *The American Language* (fourth edition, Raven McDavid, ed.). Alfred A. Knopf, 1980.

Miller, Merle. *Plain Speaking: An Oral Biography of Harry S. Truman*. Berkeley, 1973, 1974.

Pemberton, William E. *Harry S. Truman: Fair Dealer and Cold Warrior*. Twayne, 1989.

Pepper, Frank S., ed. *The Wit and Wisdom of the Twentieth Century*. Peter Bedrick, 1987.

Poen, Monte M., ed. *Strictly Personal and Confidential: The Letters Harry Truman Never Mailed.* Little, Brown, 1982.

———. *Letters Home by Harry Truman.* Putnam, 1984.

Robbins, Charles. *Last of His Kind: An Informal Portrait of Harry S. Truman.* Morrow, 1979.

Settel, T. S., ed. *The Quotable Harry S. Truman.* Droke House and Berkeley, 1975.

Simpson, James B. *Best Quotes of '54, '55, '56.* Crowell, 1957.

Smith, Timothy, ed. *Merriman Smith's Book of Presidents: A White House Memoir.* Norton, 1972.

Steinberg, Alfred. *The Man From Missouri: The Life and Times of Harry S. Truman.* G. P. Putnam's Sons, 1962.

Thompson, Kenneth W., ed. *Portraits of American Presidents: The Truman Presidency.* University Press of America, 1984.

Truman, Harry S. *Public Papers of the Presidents of the United States. Harry S. Truman. Containing the Public Messages, Speeches and Statements of the President.* U.S. Government Printing Office, 1945–1953.

———. *Memoirs, Vol. 1. Year of Decisions.* Doubleday, 1955.

———. *Memoirs, Vol. 2. Years of Trial and Hope.* Doubleday, 1956.

———. *Mr. Citizen.* Geis, 1960a.

———. *Truman Speaks.* Columbia University Press, 1960b.

———. "My First Eighty Years." *Saturday Evening Post,* June 13, 1964.

Truman, Margaret. *Harry S. Truman.* Morrow, 1973.

———, ed. *Letters from Father.* Arbor House, 1981.

———. *Bess W. Truman.* Macmillan, 1986.

———, ed. *Where the Buck Stops: The Personal and Private Writings of Harry S. Truman.* Warner, 1989.

Vernon, Laura, ed. *Harry Truman Slept Here.* Posy, 1987.

West, J. B. *Upstairs at the White House.* Coward, McCann & Geohegan, 1973.

White, William. *The Responsibles.* Harper & Row, 1972.

Williams, Herbert Lee. *The Newspaperman's President—Harry S. Truman.* Nelson-Hall, 1984.